D0116698

Heritage Edition

The
Cheyenne

Indians
of North
America

Heritage Edition

◀Indians▶
of North
◀America▶

The Apache

The Arapaho

The Blackfeet

The Cherokees

The Cheyenne

The Choctaw

The Comanche

The Hopi

The Iroquois

The Mohawk

The Navajo

The Pawnee

The Teton Sioux

The Zuni

Heritage Edition

◀ Indians ▶
of North
America

The Cheyenne

Stan Hoig
with additional text
by Paul Rosier

Foreword by
Ada E. Deer
University of Wisconsin-Madison

CHELSEA HOUSE
PUBLISHERS

COVER: Nineteenth-century Southern Cheyenne warrior's shirt.

CHELSEA HOUSE PUBLISHERS

VP, NEW PRODUCT DEVELOPMENT   Sally Cheney
DIRECTOR OF PRODUCTION   Kim Shinners
CREATIVE MANAGER   Takeshi Takahashi
MANUFACTURING MANAGER   Diann Grasse

Staff for THE CHEYENNE

EXECUTIVE EDITOR   Lee Marcott
EDITOR   Christian Green
PRODUCTION EDITOR   Bonnie Cohen
PHOTO EDITOR   Sarah Bloom
SERIES AND COVER DESIGNER   Keith Trego
LAYOUT   EJB Publishing Services

www.chelseahouse.com
First Printing

9 8 7 6 5 4 3 2 1

Library of Congress Cataloging-in-Publication Data

Hoig, Stan.
  The Cheyenne / Stan Hoig ; with additional text written by Paul Rosier.
      p. cm. — (Indians of North America (Heritage ed.))
  Includes bibliographical references and index.
  ISBN 0-7910-8598-8 (hard cover)
  1. Cheyenne Indians. I. Rosier, Paul. II. Title. III. Indians of North America (Chelsea
House Publishers : Heritage ed.)
  E99.C53H62 2005
  973.04'973—dc22
                                        2005012560

Contents

Foreword by Ada E. Deer   vi

1 An Early Glimpse   1

2 Men and Women, War and Peace   8

3 Friends and Enemies   21

4 Through the Eyes of Whites   30

5 Massacre on Sand Creek   44

6 Losing Battles   55

7 The Last Stand   68

8 Agency Life   82

9 The Tsetschestahase in the Twenty-First Century   94

The Cheyennes at a Glance   114

Chronology   115

Glossary   117

Bibliography and Further Reading   120

Index   122

Foreword

Ada E. Deer

American Indians are an integral part of our nation's life and history. Yet most Americans think of their Indian neighbors as stereotypes; they are woefully uninformed about them as fellow humans. They know little about the history, culture, and contributions of Native people. In this new millennium, it is essential for every American to know, understand, and share in our common heritage. The Cherokee teacher, the Mohawk steelworker, and the Ojibwe writer all express their tribal heritage while living in mainstream America.

The revised INDIANS OF NORTH AMERICA series, which focuses on some of the continent's larger tribes, provides the reader with an accurate perspective that will better equip him/her to live and work in today's world. Each tribe has a unique history and culture, and knowledge of individual tribes is essential to understanding the Indian experience.

Prior to the arrival of Columbus in 1492, scholars estimate the Native population north of the Rio Grande ranged from seven to twenty-five million people who spoke more than three hundred different languages. It has been estimated that ninety percent of the Native population was wiped out by disease, war, relocation, and starvation. Today there are more than 567 tribes, which have a total population of more than two million. When Columbus arrived in the Bahamas, the Arawak Indians greeted him with gifts, friendship, and hospitality. He noted their ignorance of guns and swords and wrote they could easily be overtaken with fifty men and made to do whatever he wished. This unresolved clash in perspectives continues to this day.

A holistic view recognizing the connections of all people, the land, and animals pervades the life and thinking of Native people. These core values—respect for each other and all living things; honoring the elders; caring, sharing, and living in balance with nature; and using not abusing the land and its resources—have sustained Native people for thousands of years.

American Indians are recognized in the U.S. Constitution. They are the only group in this country who has a distinctive *political* relationship with the federal government. This relationship is based on the U.S. Constitution, treaties, court decisions, and attorney-general opinions. Through the treaty process, millions of acres of land were ceded *to* the U.S. government *by* the tribes. In return, the United States agreed to provide protection, health care, education, and other services. All 377 treaties were broken by the United States. Yet treaties are the supreme law of the land as stated in the U.S. Constitution and are still valid. Treaties made more than one hundred years ago uphold tribal rights to hunt, fish, and gather.

Since 1778, when the first treaty was signed with the Lenni-Lenape, tribal sovereignty has been recognized and a government-to-government relationship was established. This concept of tribal power and authority has continuously been misunderstood by the general public and undermined by the states. In a series of court decisions in the 1830s, Chief Justice John Marshall described tribes as "domestic dependent nations." This status is not easily understood by most people and is rejected by state governments who often ignore and/or challenge tribal sovereignty. Sadly, many individual Indians and tribal governments do not understand the powers and limitations of tribal sovereignty. An overarching fact is that Congress has plenary, or absolute, power over Indians and can exercise this sweeping power at any time. Thus, sovereignty is tenuous.

Since the July 8, 1970, message President Richard Nixon issued to Congress in which he emphasized "self-determination without termination," tribes have re-emerged and have utilized the opportunities presented by the passage of major legislation such as the American Indian Tribal College Act (1971), Indian Education Act (1972), Indian Education and Self-Determination Act (1975), American Indian Health Care Improvement Act (1976), Indian Child Welfare Act (1978), American Indian Religious Freedom Act (1978), Indian Gaming Regulatory Act (1988), and Native American Graves Preservation and Repatriation Act (1990). Each of these laws has enabled tribes to exercise many facets of their sovereignty and consequently has resulted in many clashes and controversies with the states and the general public. However, tribes now have more access to and can afford attorneys to protect their rights and assets.

Under provisions of these laws, many Indian tribes reclaimed power over their children's education with the establishment of tribal schools and thirty-one tribal colleges. Many Indian children have been rescued from the foster-care system. More tribal people are freely practicing their traditional religions. Tribes with gaming revenue have raised their standard of living with improved housing, schools, health clinics, and other benefits. Ancestors' bones have been reclaimed and properly buried. All of these laws affect and involve the federal, state, and local governments as well as individual citizens.

Tribes are no longer people of the past. They are major players in today's economic and political arenas; contributing millions of dollars to the states under the gaming compacts and supporting political candidates. Each of the tribes in INDIANS OF NORTH AMERICA demonstrates remarkable endurance, strength, and adaptability. They are buying land, teaching their language and culture, and creating and expanding their economic base, while developing their people and making decisions for future generations. Tribes will continue to exist, survive, and thrive.

Ada E. Deer
University of Wisconsin–Madison
June 2004

1

An Early Glimpse

In 1806 a small band of mounted Cheyenne warriors arrived at the great bend of the Missouri River in what is now North Dakota. They had come to visit the Mandans and the Hidatsas (called *Gros Ventres*, or Big Bellies by French traders), members of the Missouri River Indian federation who lived in villages composed of rounded mud huts. The Cheyennes, long at war with these two bands, now wanted to establish a peaceful trading relationship with them. As a gesture of goodwill, the Cheyennes invited the Mandans and the Hidatsas to send a delegation to the Cheyenne encampment near the Black Hills of South Dakota, where they could exchange corn, squash, and other produce for splendid Cheyenne horses. The Cheyennes offered to return to the Hidatsas a young boy they had captured in battle and held hostage for several years.

Some of the Mandans and the Hidatsas suspected treachery. In the past the Cheyennes had been aggressive and combative, and there was no reason to believe they had suddenly changed their ways. After some debate, however, the two bands accepted the Cheyenne offer and agreed to send a trading caravan to the Cheyenne encampment. Village leaders asked a visitor, Charles Mackenzie, a trader from Canada, to join the expedition and promised him two horse loads of furs as payment. Mackenzie agreed. Alexander Henry, another Canadian trader, also went along.

Fortunately, both men wrote excellent accounts of the meeting between these Indian *tribes*. They described, among other things, the imposing caravan that set out for the Cheyenne camp. It was led by a mounted Hidatsa chief. He held a long staff that flew an American flag as a sign of peace. It had been presented to the band in 1804 by American explorers Meriwether Lewis and William Clark during their historic trek to the Pacific Ocean.

The Hidatsa chief was flanked by two mounted war leaders. Next, in tight formation, came foot soldiers, eight squads of thirty to forty young warriors. Each wore gaudy paint and feathers, and they were equipped with bows, arrows, lances, battle-axes, and shields. As they marched, these warriors shook rattles made of red deer hooves and at intervals sang and shouted. Behind them followed a group of older men, and in the rear walked women and children bearing provisions. All told, the expedition included more than nine hundred people.

For five days they traveled south, crossing three rivers—the Clearwater, the Heart, and the Cannonball—into Cheyenne territory. In the report Mackenzie filed with the North West Trading Company, he described the abundant wildlife he saw:

> Immense herds of buffaloes quench[ed] their thirst at these rivers and repos[ed] on their banks. . . . There were numerous flocks of red and fallow deer, the most of which, in the height of the day, were lying on the sides of the hills, while others were on the watch sniffing the fresh breeze while

Like all Plains Indians, the Cheyennes relied on the buffalo to provide food, clothing, and shelter. Herds like this one were once so numerous that early explorers to the Great Plains often could not count them. It is estimated that there were once 60 million buffalo in the United States, but by the late 1800s their numbers had declined to a few hundred.

their companions indulged in a watchful slumber. There were also several muddy creeks, with a little water here and there, which the beavers had conserved by stopping the course of the outlets.

On the morning of the sixth day, the trading caravan came upon the Cheyennes. They saw first a solid wall of horsemen, more than one hundred strong. Each horseman brandished brightly feathered shields and lances draped with scalp locks. The warriors' high-spirited horses came from huge herds tended by the Cheyennes on meadows near their camp. The

visitors noted the animals' size and strength and their frighten-
ing masks, which resembled the heads of wild beasts. Red cloth
trimmed their mouths and nostrils, giving them a demonic
appearance. Behind this formidable wall of horses and riders
stood the Cheyenne foot soldiers.

It was a tense moment as the old enemies, both assembled
in large numbers, silently faced one another. All eyes turned
toward a handsome black stallion mounted by an imposing war
leader clad in a blue coat and a striped blanket of Spanish
make. The warrior suddenly pressed his horse into a gallop and
sped toward the American flag held forward by the Hidatsas.
The Cheyenne warrior accepted the proffered banner and
embraced the chief. All the other Cheyennes then rode forward
to greet their visitors and lead them toward their camp.

Outside the Cheyenne camp lay stacks of long, barkless
poles used to make *travois*—vehicles that could be loaded with
goods and dragged by dogs or horses. The hub of the camp
consisted of a horseshoe-shaped arrangement of some 120
tepees—cone-shaped lodges made of buffalo hides. Their cross-
poles, poking through a circle at the top, glistened in the morning sun. Long strips of buffalo meat hung drying on racks.
Black-haired Cheyenne women busied themselves with various
tasks. Some stretched and pegged hides onto the ground; others dressed buffalo robes or worked the pelts of smaller game
with straw and porcupine quills.

Upon entering the camp, the visitors received a warm wel-
come—at first. Then more newcomers arrived, a small band of
Assiniboines (a Canadian border tribe) that had trailed the
expedition. The Hidatsas and Mandans greeted these surprise
guests hospitably, but their hosts were furious. The Cheyennes
held a long-standing grudge against the Assiniboines, who in
years past had destroyed Cheyenne villages. The Cheyennes
wanted to kill the newcomers, but their visitors resisted. The
goodwill of the Cheyennes dissolved into sullen anger. They
remained hostile throughout the meeting.

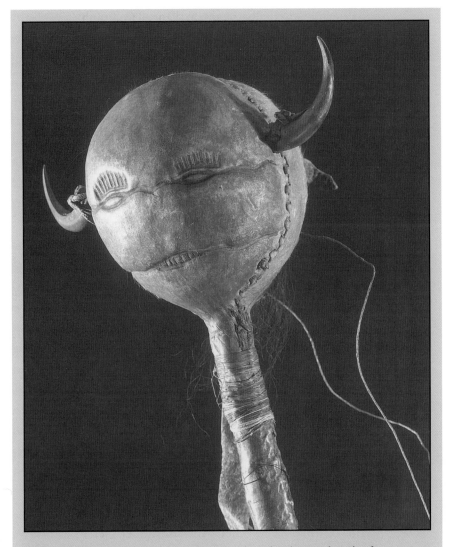

Rattles such as this one—which is adorned with eagle talons and made of rawhide—were often used by the Cheyennes in ceremonies and in preparation for battle.

Even the promised return of the Gros Ventre boy went off badly. The procedure for recovering the captive involved a ceremony that featured the *calumet,* a long-stemmed pipe with a red clay head and ornaments of feather and scalp locks. The calumet was placed on a length of red cloth by a Gros Ventre priest, while other tribe members danced and sang to the beating of drums and shaking of rattles. After this a buffalo skull, its eyes and nostrils stuffed with hay, was placed on an offering shroud—an altar heaped with guns and ammunition presented as gifts. Custom called for the Cheyennes to respond by offering horses. They held back their fine mounts and instead brought forth only lame and scabby nags. At last, they presented the captive boy, wrapped in the American flag, but the ritual abruptly concluded without further ceremony. Fearful that blood might be spilled, the Gros Ventres and Mandans made a cautious retreat from the Cheyenne camp.

The account of this episode by Mackenzie and Henry was the first by whites to provide an in-depth view of the Cheyennes at the height of their power, when the tribe roamed freely on the Great Plains. Before then—in fact, as late as the seventeenth century—the Cheyennes lived west of the Great Lakes, probably in what is now northern Minnesota. In the late seventeenth century, the tribe migrated farther west and settled on the Red River of the North, where it serves as the border between the present-day states of Minnesota and North Dakota. Soon they established contacts with the Mandan, Gros Ventre, and other tribes. Like them, the Cheyennes built villages made of earthen dwellings and became farmers, growing corn, beans, and squash.

Cheyenne culture changed dramatically in the late eighteenth century when other tribes introduced them to horses, which had been brought to the New World by Spanish explorers. By 1830, the tribe had become master horse breeders and riders. They forsook farming for hunting and abandoned permanent village life for the nomadic existence appropriate to the pursuit of the large herds of bison, or buffalo, that roamed the grassy prairies of the Great Plains. As a result, the Cheyennes became a major presence in a vast area of the American West, ranging as far south as New Mexico and as far north as Montana.

In these same years—the mid-nineteenth century—the United States began to expand its borders westward. Traders, immigrants, and the U.S. Army steadily streamed into the open wilds the Cheyennes considered their own. The tribe tried to drive off these intruders, but they were too numerous, and the Cheyennes became resigned to sharing their land with the U.S. government. Sadly, even this arrangement failed, as the huge buffalo herds—the tribe's staple game—were slaughtered wholesale by white hunters. Inevitably, the differences between two opposing cultures led to armed conflict. From 1857 to 1879, the Cheyennes fought an ongoing war with the U.S. Army. The tribe won some battles, including the celebrated battle at Little Bighorn, where they helped the Sioux fight Lieutenant Colonel George Armstrong Custer and his troops in 1876.

In the end, though, the Cheyennes had no chance of defeating so powerful a foe, and in the 1880s they surrendered and accepted removal to reservations. Some Cheyennes ended up in *Indian Territory* (present-day Oklahoma); others went to Montana. They remain there to this day, where they struggle to preserve their own rich heritage despite the demands of the larger society that rules them. That struggle echoes with the remembrance of a long and glorious history.

2

Men and Women, War and Peace

The first contact between whites and the Cheyennes occurred in 1680 when a group of Indians visited the French explorer René-Robert Cavelier, Sieur de La Salle while he was building Fort Crevecoeur on the Illinois River. These people spoke the tongue of the *Algonkian*, who populated a vast region north of the Great Lakes and called themselves *Tsis-tsis'-tas*, or "the People."

At this time the tribe was known as the Chaa. They resided on the banks of the Minnesota River in earth-covered lodges. A peaceful people, they made pottery and ate small deer, rabbits, fish, bird eggs, berries, and roots. The Chaas remained in this area until the early eighteenth century, when a larger nation, the Sioux, pushed them west into North Dakota. There they settled along another river, the Sheyenne, and built earth-lodge villages. They became planters, raising corn, beans, and squash.

Throughout these years, the Cheyennes were a sedentary,

peaceful people. They suffered attacks from larger tribes, such as the Cree, Ojibway, Sioux, and the Assiniboine, who overran and badly mauled them in approximately 1740. The few survivors fled southwest across the Missouri River and near the Black Hills of South Dakota. One band was massacred by a large party of Sioux.

Also at this time, the Cheyennes acquired horses, which had been brought north from the Great Plains by the Comanche, Kiowa, and other tribes. Horses changed the culture of the Cheyennes in two crucial ways. First, Cheyenne men, often tall and lithe, adapted so effectively to mounted battle that they quickly became among the most feared of all Indian warriors. They now were a match for larger tribes that had formerly defeated them. Second, the Cheyennes became highly skilled hunters. Previously, they had been hampered by a lack of mobility in their pursuit of the buffalo, mainly because when they didn't have horses, the entire band had to form a "surround," driving the animals into a small area where they could be trapped and killed. Horses enabled individual Cheyenne hunters to easily pursue the buffalo.

The Cheyennes began to hunt the game that roamed in huge herds across the Great Plains, especially the buffalo, which proved invaluable to them. Their meat and the chunky tallow fat provided food in both winter and summer. Buffalo hide could be tanned into leather for ropes, horse gear, and other essential goods. Buffalo skin also furnished the coverings for a new kind of abode—tepees (introduced to the Cheyennes by the Sioux). These dwellings featured a central fire, and along the sides were beds made of thick, matted robes (also taken from the buffalo) that provided warmth against the bitter cold of winter. Because tepees were portable, they enabled Cheyenne warriors to take their families with them rather than leave them behind in unprotected villages when they ventured onto the plains.

The Cheyennes prospered on the plains. Their population

grew, and they gained strength through alliances with the Arapahos and the Sioux. By the end of the eighteenth century, the Cheyennes had begun warring with other tribes of the northern plains. No written accounts of their early conquests exist, but Mandan robes decorated with symbolic artwork often include depictions of battles with Cheyenne warriors.

The Mandans were not their only foes. Cheyenne war parties riding westward came into conflict with the Crows, who lived in the Bighorn River country of Wyoming and Montana; the Shoshones, who lived along the Sweetwater River in Wyoming; and the Utes, who inhabited the eastern slopes of the Rocky Mountains in Colorado. In addition, the Cheyennes helped defeat the Kiowas and drive them south from their home along the North Platte River of Wyoming and Nebraska.

"These lands once belonged to the Kiowas and the Crows," Black Hawk, an Oglala Sioux chief, once boasted to United States peace commissioners, "but we whipped these nations out of them. We met the Kiowas and whipped them, at the Kiowa Creek, just below where we now are. We met them and whipped them again and the last time at Crow Creek. This last battle was fought by the Cheyennes, Arapahos and Ogallahlahs [Oglala] combined." The Cheyennes' most persistent enemy were the Pawnees, who lived along the Loup River in Nebraska. The prize in this contest was an extensive buffalo range that covered western Kansas and Nebraska. In their effort to protect their claim to this area, the Pawnees, often allied with eastern tribes such as the Sac, Fox, and Delaware. The Cheyennes, for their part, teamed up with their Arapaho confederates. Buffalo were not the only goal. The Cheyennes also invaded the ranges south of the Arkansas River to raid the enormous horse herds owned by the Comanche and other tribes.

In the nineteenth century, Cheyenne culture featured three dangerous activities, each a test of bravery and skill: hunting, horse stealing, and fighting. At an early age, males learned that status within the tribe was linked to the ability to handle weapons and stalk prey. Cheyenne men hunted all sorts of game, including large animals such as antelope, deer, elk, wild sheep, and, of course, buffalo. They also tracked down smaller beasts, especially wolves and foxes for their fur. Buffalo remained their staple, however, and the Cheyennes refined techniques for hunting them. The hunter spent long hours training his horse to ride close to the animal, so that both his hands would be free to use his bow and arrow. A powerful hunter could shoot an arrow so forcefully that it passed cleanly through one buffalo and penetrated the hide of another. Spears also made good weapons for killing buffalo.

Horses were valuable to the Cheyennes. Without them one could not cover the vast stretches of the prairie. A good war pony was easily a man's most precious possession. The Cheyennes procured the animals any way they could. Warriors raided the fleet herds that raced across the southern ranges. An even greater feat was stealing horses from other tribes. Plains Indians viewed this thievery not as a crime but as a noble deed that required courage and skill.

The Cheyennes vied with other tribes that hunted the buffalo on the Great Plains. Warriors developed ways of measuring their prowess, in order to win respect within the tribe. One test was *counting coup*, wherein the warrior touched his enemy with a long, crook-ended stick. Like scalp taking, this form of conquest enabled a young warrior to make his mark within the tribe. Coups earned him the admiration of the entire band. When warriors returned to the domestic world of the camp, everyone—including eligible young women—turned out to celebrate their war exploits.

The Cheyennes also paid tribute to war skills through five military societies—Fox, Elk, Shield, Dog, and *Bowstring*. Each club had its own distinctive style of dress and its own dances and songs. In organization, however, all the clubs were similar. Each, for instance, had four leaders: Two acted as war chiefs and decision makers; two served as messengers and ambassadors to the other clubs and to the tribe's peace leaders. One military society, the *Dog Soldiers*, became the most notorious, and its members were the most feared warriors on the Great Plains in the nineteenth century, when the Cheyennes battled the expanding republic of the United States. The Dog Soldiers came to constitute a band of their own, the only one whose membership was restricted to certain *clans*, a group of Indians tracing their descent to a common ancestor.

Although the Cheyennes were accomplished warriors, the most esteemed members of their tribe were their chiefs, who were responsible for peace within the tribe and with outside nations. A Cheyenne chief usually had distinguished himself as a warrior but prided himself in his ability to maintain harmony for his people. Each chief was chosen for a ten-year term that could not be revoked for any reason.

Chiefs had to be exemplary men—calm, generous, kind, sympathetic, courageous, and self-sacrificing. They routinely lavished gifts on the poor and unfortunate, even on enemies. In *The Cheyenne Way*, a study published in 1941, researchers K.N. Llewellyn and E.A. Hoebel cite the example of High-backed Wolf, a chief who once came upon a Pawnee beaten and left naked by Cheyenne warriors. "I am going to help you out," the chief announced to the stricken man. "Here are your clothes. Outside are three horses. You may take your choice! Here is a mountain lion skin."

As anthropologist G.B. Grinnell wrote in his 1923 book, *The Cheyenne Indians: Their History and Way of Life*: "A good chief gave his whole heart and his whole mind to the work of helping his people, and strove for their welfare with an earnestness and a devotion rarely equaled by the rulers of other men. . . . True friends, delightful companions, wise counselors, they were men whose attitude toward their fellows we might all emulate." Their compassion sometimes exceeded the bounds of reason. A chief would not protest when another man ran off with his wife; he might even refuse the compensation offered

High-backed Wolf, depicted here in an 1832 painting by renowned frontier artist George Catlin, was one of several Cheyenne war chiefs who signed the first treaty—the Treaty of 1825—between the United States and the Cheyennes.

by the culprit—a pipe, horse, and other gifts—because to accept them was to admit being wounded by the loss, which would dent the chief's dignity.

At any time, forty-four chiefs—four from each of their ten bands plus the four principal chiefs—formed the council that governed the entire Cheyenne nation. Within this council, four chiefs attained a special status that combined governmental and religious functions. First came the head priest-chief, called the Sweet Medicine Chief. He was entrusted with a sacred package of grass—the Sweet Medicine Bundle—that he inherited from his predecessor and passed on to his successor. During meetings in the council tepee, or lodge, he occupied a special seat called *heum* (meaning "the above"). It signified that he was the mortal representative of the deity who ruled the earth, itself symbolized by the circle scooped out of the ground at the foot of his ceremonial seat.

This circle was surrounded by sticks. One corresponded to Sweet Medicine Chief, and the other sticks corresponded to the other leading chiefs. These men represented divine spirits such as the Big Holy People, or Those Who Know Everything; Where the Food Comes From; and the Spirit Who Gives Good Health. Thus, these chiefs were emissaries of the benevolent forces that ruled Cheyenne life.

At council meetings, the chiefs decided various issues, such as whether to move camp or to form alliances with other tribes. The council also resolved judicial matters. They decreed what punishment should be meted out to lawbreakers and resolved feuds that threatened the harmony of the tribe. Each meeting began with several minutes of silence. Then one of the oldest, most experienced men introduced an issue for debate. No one ever interrupted another speaker, and all men freely voiced their views. In summer, the sides of the tepee were rolled up, and a large audience might gather to hear the deliberations. Once a decision was reached, the chiefs informed their bands and explained what action would be taken and why.

Hunting, thieving, warring, and lawmaking fell to men, but much that was essential to Cheyenne culture was the province of women, who ruled the all-important domestic sphere. One major chore was gathering the food for the family. This was often no easy task. A favorite vegetable, turnips, had to be dug out of the ground, boiled, sliced, and then dried in the sun. Even more difficult was the process of collecting the fruit that

Tools such as this buffalo hide scraper, which is made from a bison femur bone, were used by Cheyenne women to remove hides from the body of the buffalo so that they could make clothing, including dresses, shirts, moccasins, and leggings.

sprouted on the prickly pear cactus. First, women yanked clumps of fruit off the plant and stuck them in a *parfleche* (rawhide bag). Next, they brushed away the spines with brooms made of twigs. Then, with their fingers protected by deerskin thimbles, they carefully picked the fruit clean. Finally, they separated the seeds and dried the rest in the sun. The result was a tasty thickener for stews and soups.

Women spent most of their time fixing meals, tanning hides, and sewing clothing. When the band moved camp, women rolled up the hide walls of the tepee and—when the band resettled—rolled them back down. If it seemed the site would be permanent, women modeled their tepees into comfortable homes, with raised mats, grass-covered "benches" (made of sod), and cupboards ingeniously formed of buffalo robes. The work women did on their dwellings was prized by the entire band, and no man could cross the threshold of a new tepee until a brave warrior first stepped into it and was followed by other esteemed men.

The many chores performed by Cheyenne women required a variety of tools that they made themselves. One was a stone maul, or hammer, with a willow-branch handle. It was used to pound tepee pegs into the ground, chop firewood, and shatter animal bones for soup. Women also kept several spoons made of steamed or boiled horns removed from slain buffalo or sheep. Every Cheyenne woman owned a set of tools for tanning, the painstaking process whereby tough animal hide was softened into pliable material.

Once hide was tanned and dried, women sewed it into garments. For themselves they fashioned several skins into long dresses that hung below the knee. For men they made long-sleeved shirts, fringed leggings, and breechcloths—square skins tied around the waist with a cord. Men and women alike wore moccasins, which had rawhide soles and were beautifully embellished with beads. The most elaborate clothing of all was the decorated, or quilled, robe. To make one, a woman needed the sponsorship of the *Quillers' Society*, an exclusive club, like the military societies. Its members instructed others and obeyed hallowed rituals, such as delivering recitations in which they named the best garments they had ever sewn.

One of the most remarkable qualities exhibited by Cheyenne women was their chastity. Traders and travelers often praised their modesty and diffidence, and Cheyenne men honored them for it. A suitor might wait five years before his beloved would agree to marry him. He would not dream of embarrassing her by posing the question directly. Instead, he enlisted an aged relative—often a woman—who approached the girl's family with gifts. After stating the young man's case,

A group of Cheyenne men gather outside a lodge in Oklahoma in preparation for the Sun Dance. The dance, which traditionally ran for eight days in May, symbolized the renewal of the world and involved fasting and self-torture.

she promptly left the family alone to discuss the matter privately. The next day, they announced their decision.

If the marriage was approved, the bride was clad in her loveliest buckskin dress, placed upon the finest horse owned by her family, and led by an old woman—never a relative—to the house of the groom. His relatives lifted the bride off the horse, set her on a ceremonial blanket, and then carried her across the threshold. The groom's female relatives clothed her in new finery, dressed her hair, and painted her face. The ceremony concluded with a feast. Afterward, the bride's mother supplied the couple with a new tepee and furnishings, and both families contributed household items. The newlyweds took up residence near the bride's home. Prosperous men might take several wives, each of whom belonged to his extended family, and each inhabiting her own tepee with her children. The marriage ceremony was only one of many observed by the Cheyennes.

Their culture included a larger body of social lore, some of it adopted from other tribes, some uniquely their own. One such unique ceremony was the *Renewal of the Medicine* (or Sacred) *Arrows.* It developed after the tribe underwent the great societal change created when they became hunters and warriors. The ceremony fell on the longest day of the year. On this day, the entire tribe—all ten bands—moved to an open area watered by a stream and placed their tepees in a wide circle. Within the circle stood the lodge of the Keeper of the Arrows, and in the exact center stood a huge tepee, the Sacred Arrow Lodge. Inside it,

The Sun Dance Ceremony

The Cheyenne and other Plains Indian tribes performed the Sun Dance in order to revitalize and replenish the natural world with earth, water, wind, and herds of buffalo.

According to tribal tradition, the Sun Dance originated during a time of famine among the Cheyennes. In order to alleviate the suffering of his people, a Cheyenne named Erect Horns and his wife made a pilgrimage to the Sacred Mountain to seek guidance from the Great Spirit. The Great Spirit told Erect Horns that he must sponsor a Sun Dance, and he instructed him in the intricacies of the ceremony. Ever since, Sun Dances have become a regular part of Cheyenne ritual.

The ceremony begins when a male member of the tribe—sometimes called "The Multiplier" or "The Reproducer" because the tribe is reborn through his act of generosity—announces that he is organizing the ceremony. The sponsor then retreats with his wife and the tribal priests into the Lone Tepee, raised as a symbol of the Sacred Mountain.

For four days those isolated inside the Lone Tepee symbolically reenact Erect Horns' visit to the Great Spirit. They also perform sacred rites of regeneration, such as shaping the tepee's dirt floor into five mounds (each symbolizing the earth). On the fourth day, the priests consecrate a buffalo skull, thereby guaranteeing that the herds will abound for the rest of the year.

priests opened a bundle that held the arrows. Cheyenne belief held that two of these arrows, when aimed at the buffalo, reduced the beasts to powerlessness, and that the other two arrows had the same effect on human enemies. After the conclusion of the Renewal Ceremony, all the participants purified themselves in a lodge before they could resume their role in ordinary life.

Cheyenne rituals also included several dances. One, the *Sun Dance*, was practiced by a number of Plains Indian tribes. It lasted eight days and was highlighted by a dance performed by

During the four days of Lone Tepee rites, the rest of the camp gathers to build a Sun Dance lodge, a central pole encircled by a ring of upright wooden posts, all joined at the top by long, horizontal strips of timber. The Cheyennes then cover this structure with the buffalo robes of celebrated warriors. When the priests emerge from the Lone Tepee, they bless the lodge and offer prayers to the Great Spirit.

The dance itself begins when warriors—their faces decorated with ceremonial paint—gather around the lodge's central pole and rise repeatedly up and down on their toes, blowing through eagle-bone whistles held between their teeth. They repeat this activity for four days and usually do not stop to eat and drink.

After the dancing ends, Cheyenne warriors conclude the Sun Dance with ritual torture. Several men pierce the faces, chests, or backs of their comrades with sharpened skewers. This painful ceremony is thought to arouse the pity of spirits. Yet it is also an important rite of passage for males, an occasion for them to display publicly their bravery and capacity to endure pain. After the eight-day ceremony concludes, the Cheyennes leave the Sun Dance lodge confident that they have revitalized the natural world around them.

young men whose chests were implanted with leather thongs tethered to a lodge pole. These torturous conditions tested the warriors' tolerance of extreme physical pain. A second dance included men and women dressed as animals. They performed zany, or *massa'ne*, antics as they tried to elude hunters who belonged to the Bowstring Society.

Cheyenne religious beliefs influenced their relationship with whites, whom they regarded with superstition, possibly because of an incident that occurred in 1795. That year "the Lance," a Cheyenne chief, accepted gifts from a French trader and promised, in return, to treat strangers hospitably. The Lance broke his vow and murdered a Sioux and his family living among the Cheyennes. Soon after, three of the Lance's children died. Next, lightning struck the hut inhabited by his brother, who was killed along with his family and even his dogs and horses.

The Cheyennes developed the belief that white people were bad omens. A typical incident occurred in 1804, when the Lewis and Clark expedition met them at a Mandan village while en route to the Pacific Ocean. As a token of friendship, Captain Clark offered a Cheyenne chief the gift of a small medal. Instead of being pleased, the chief grew alarmed. He explained that, in his view, white people were "medicine" and therefore must be shown homage. He accepted the gift only after Clark consented to accept a robe and buffalo meat in exchange. Eventually, the Cheyennes would find more concrete reasons for distrusting whites.

3

Friends and Enemies

In the early 1800s, the Cheyennes resided on the Cheyenne River near the Black Hills, although they had begun to winter in Colorado near the headwaters of two large rivers. One, the South Platte, ran east; the other, the Arkansas, emptied into the Mississippi River. The Cheyennes headed south for several reasons: to spend the winter in a warmer climate, to raid the huge herds of wild horses kept by some southern tribes, and to hunt bear and beaver, which filled the southern edge of the Rocky Mountains in north-central Colorado, near present-day Denver. With the arrival of spring, the Cheyennes returned north to trade their skins and horses to the Missouri River tribes or to white traders.

Soon the Cheyennes began a larger migration, one that relocated much of the tribe. The way was opened in the eighteenth century, when the large Comanche nation moved from the northern Rockies into the horse-rich lower plains and forced the Apaches south. In the wake of the Comanches came the Kiowas. These tribes ultimately became allied and formed a single entity. Their departure from the high plains east of the Rockies left a vacuum into which the Cheyennes moved. Initially, they ventured south on only a temporary basis: As late as 1825, the majority of the Cheyenne population still lived near the Black Hills. About this time, the tribe separated into two groups. Some Cheyenne bands preferred the northern country; others began to take up permanent residence along the Arkansas River in southern Colorado. There was no enmity between the two groups; they maintained their clan and family contacts but they pulled apart: The Southern Cheyennes remained in their new home, and the Northern Cheyennes roamed west from the Black Hills to the high country of Wyoming and Montana along the North Platte, the Powder, and the Tongue rivers. As time passed, the split became more distinct.

In 1828, the Southern Cheyennes found a powerful incentive to remain in Colorado. That year, Missourians Charles and William Bent, trappers and traders, had a fateful encounter with a party of Cheyennes who had come south to catch wild horses. The Cheyenne party was led by Yellow Wolf, a highly intelligent chief. The Bents proposed opening regular trade relations with Yellow Wolf. The chief agreed and suggested that the white men locate downriver from the mountains and away from the buffalo range. If they would do so, he said, he would bring his band and others there to trade.

Accordingly, in 1883, the Bents constructed a log-and-*adobe* mud fort at the point where the Arkansas and Purgatoire rivers converge in the flatlands of southeastern Colorado. Later known as Fort William, or Bent's Fort, this permanent trading post became a stopping place for countless whites who traversed the plains along the Santa Fe Trail, the pioneer route that reached from Missouri to New Mexico. Many famous men of the West would be associated with Bent's Fort, including Kit Carson, who was a Bent trader for a time before becoming a

George Bent, shown here with his Cheyenne wife Magpie, lived for many years among the Cheyennes. George was the son of Owl Woman and William Bent, who, along with his brother, Charles, had set up a trading post (Bent's Fort) in 1833 at the confluence of the Arkansas and Purgatoire rivers in southeastern Colorado, where they traded with the Cheyenne and other Indian tribes.

Western explorer, guide, and U.S. Army scout. The Bents themselves went on to accomplish a great deal in the West. Charles Bent was appointed governor of New Mexico Territory, and William married a Cheyenne woman, had children by her, and became deeply involved in frontier Indian affairs.

The construction of Bent's Fort signaled the beginning of a

new phase of Cheyenne history, as whites began to encroach on the Great Plains. For the time being, however, the Cheyennes welcomed Bent's Fort and the steady traffic of immigrants who journeyed along the Arkansas River. Mexicans trekked up from Taos, in present-day New Mexico, and American and French traders arrived. These men regularly visited and sometimes lived among the Cheyennes, bringing them goods from the outside world.

Not long before the Bents set up their trading post, the Cheyennes formally met official representatives of the United States. This episode occurred in June 1820, when the U.S. government sent a group of nineteen mounted Americans led by Stephen H. Long on an expedition up the Missouri and Platte rivers. Long explored as far west as the Rocky Mountains, contacting Indians living in the region. The party divided when it reached the Arkansas River. Long took nine of the men south to explore the headwaters of the Red River. Captain J. R. Bell led the others on a return trip along the Arkansas and met a party of Cheyennes near the mouth of the Purgatoire River.

In 1825, when the majority of the Cheyennes still lived near the Black Hills, they were visited by General Henry Atkinson and U.S. Indian agent Benjamin O'Fallon, who had been appointed by President James Monroe to sign treaties with the tribes they encountered. The emissaries were escorted by 476 U.S. troops sent along to impress the Indians with the power and importance of the United States.

The expedition proceeded up the Missouri River in flat-bottomed, or keel, boats fitted with manually operated paddle-wheels and also with sails and oars. The party included mounted hunters who rode along the riverbank chasing game to feed the voyagers. On July 4, 1825, at the mouth of the Teton River, Atkinson signed a *treaty* with the great Cheyenne chief High-backed Wolf, another chief (named Little Moon), and others.

By signing the Treaty of 1825, the Cheyennes acknowledged

the supremacy of the U.S. government, which, in turn, promised the tribe protection and friendship. The treaty spelled out trade agreements, included mutual guarantees of safe passage for Americans traveling through Cheyenne territory, and prohibited the sale of arms by traders to tribes unfriendly to the United States.

Atkinson's party was impressed by the Cheyennes, who seemed purer than white men. "They have unlike other Indians all the virtues that nature can give without the vices of civilization," wrote an officer in a letter to the Washington, D.C., *Daily National Intelligencer.* "They are artless, fearless, and live in constant exercise of moral and Christian virtues, though they know it not."

Another member of Atkinson's party, a journalist, noted that High-backed Wolf was one of the most dignified and elegant-looking men he had ever seen. This opinion was echoed by artist George Catlin, who painted portraits of both the chief and his wife, She Who Bathes Her Knees. The painting shows High-backed Wolf dressed in an Indian deerskin suit handsomely adorned with porcupine quills. His wife wears a dress made of mountain sheepskin decorated with quills and beads. Less than a decade later, High-backed Wolf would die at the hands of his own people while trying to keep the peace in a tribal argument. The death of this great leader widened the rift between the Northern and Southern Cheyennes and encouraged the southern migration of many Cheyennes.

Even as the Cheyennes formed valuable friendships with white traders, they remained at odds with other Indians. In 1825, a party of Northern Cheyenne Bowstring warriors was massacred in a battle against the Crows on the Tongue River. The Cheyennes wanted vengeance and sent emissaries to the Sioux, who agreed to join them in raising an armed force. These warriors located a Crow camp and made a surprise attack at dawn. They overran the camp and seized many women and children as captives. Later, the Crows were permitted to visit Cheyenne villages and to recover the captives, though—as often happened—some of the Crow women had already become Cheyenne wives and mothers.

Another enemy was the Comanches, whose large horse herds were often raided by the Cheyennes. After one sortie, the Comanche chief Bull Hump led a war party that located a Cheyenne encampment in Colorado on the South Platte River. The Comanches raided their herds and headed south with a large number of horses—their own and some taken from the Cheyennes. They had reached the Arkansas River when Yellow Wolf discovered them and led his warriors in a dawn attack, stampeding the horses. A fight ensued, and the Cheyennes, armed with guns (the Comanches had only bows and arrows), forced their foes to retreat, leaving behind their horses and a few warriors.

In the late 1830s, the Southern Cheyennes battled the Pawnees after they had wiped out an entire party of Cheyenne horse thieves. The Cheyennes did not retaliate immediately. Instead they waited out the winter. When spring arrived, they "moved the Medicine Arrows"—took up arms—against the Pawnees. A large contingent of Arapahos and Sioux joined the Cheyenne offensive.

During the ensuing battle, the Keeper of the Arrows tied the sacred weapons to the head of his lance and carried them into the fight. As the opposing sides squared off, a Pawnee suffering from an illness seated himself between the lines, evidently to await his death. The Keeper of the Arrows charged at him, but the Pawnee grabbed the lance and jerked away the arrows. Several Cheyennes made a fierce charge in an attempt to recover them, but some Pawnees got to their comrade first and made off with the Medicine Arrows. The Cheyennes killed the ailing Pawnee, but the loss of the sacred arrows dampened their spirits, and they gave up the fight. The incident was followed by intense mourning at various Cheyenne camps. Women and children wailed in despair, and warriors sheared off their hair. The Cheyennes never recovered the arrows, but they got revenge in 1833 when they surrounded a Pawnee war party on foot in the hills near Bent's Fort and slaughtered every last man. The site became known as the "Pawnee Hills."

The Cheyennes continued pilfering horses from the southern Plains tribes, leading to still another clash between Yellow Wolf and Bull Hump in 1836. Following a Cheyenne raid on a Comanche herd on the north fork of the Red River, Bull Hump once again set out to recover his mounts. He and his men tracked the herd past Bent's Fort. Fortunately, he did not spot the prize stallion that Yellow Wolf had presented to William Bent. The animal was named "Yellow Wolf," and ultimately became a hunting horse for Kit Carson.

Once again the Cheyennes succeeded in stealing Comanche horses. Their luck ran out the following year when a party of forty-eight Bowstring warriors went south on foot to filch mounts from the Kiowa herds. The entire group was discovered, killed, and scalped by the Kiowas and Comanches. Yellow Wolf and other Cheyenne leaders were determined to avenge this defeat. An opportunity arose in 1838 when a combined force of Cheyenne and Arapaho warriors located a Comanche-Kiowa encampment along Wolf Creek in present-day Oklahoma. The Cheyenne-Arapaho party was discovered as it approached the Comanche-Kiowa camp and was met in force about a mile away. In a clash of charging warriors, the defenders were slowly beaten back and the village overrun. The Comanche and Kiowa women made a futile effort to survive by digging trenches in which they tried to hide with their children.

The resulting massacre halted only when the Cheyennes learned that a company of U.S. dragoons and Osage scouts was already on its way to pay the Comanches a visit. This news caused the Cheyennes to retreat. They left fourteen fallen comrades, along with fifty-eight dead Comanches and Kiowas and more than one hundred slain horses.

Bent's Fort, which is today a National Historic Site, was one of the most prominent trading posts in the West during the 1830s and '40s. Situated along the Santa Fe Trail, the fort was also host to a large peace council in 1840, in which the Cheyennes, Arapahos, Comanches, Kiowas, and Prairie Apaches agreed upon a friendship pact.

The Battle of Wolf Creek led to a large peace council in 1840. It was held at Bent's Fort and was attended by the Cheyennes, Arapahos, Comanches, Kiowas, and Prairie Apaches. After festivities that included a feast, music, singing, dancing, and an exchange of gifts, the tribes agreed upon a friendship pact. This pact granted the Cheyennes and Arapahos the privilege to range freely south of the Arkansas River.

By this time, the number of whites had risen in the Great Plains, and conflicts pitted them against the Plains Indians. In 1841, Cheyennes and Sioux clashed with a party of white trappers on the Snake River in Wyoming. In this fight, the Indians lost eight or ten warriors, and five trappers died, including their leader. A year later, explorer John Charles Frémont encountered a Cheyenne-Arapaho village on the South Platte. As Frémont rode along the irregular path that ran through the village, he noted that before most of the lodges stood birch-limb tripods bearing glistening white shields and burnished spearheads. Frémont touched one of the shields with his gun muzzle, half expecting an angry warrior to confront him.

Yet relations between the Cheyennes and whites generally remained amicable. In 1842, the same year that Frémont visited the Cheyenne village, American trader Bill Hamilton led a party into a camp of friendly Cheyennes who were willing to trade their robes and pelts for powder, balls, flints, beads, paint, blue and scarlet cloths, blankets, calico, and knives. However, dealing with white traders would eventually cause the Cheyennes great misery.

4

Through the Eyes of Whites

T he advent of white men brought many blessings to the Cheyennes. They gladly bolstered their diet with coffee, flour, sugar, and other foods. Cheyenne women lightened their domestic burdens with household items, such as pots and pans, and they enjoyed novelties such as printed cloth material, combs, mirrors, and beads. Warriors, for their part, profited from steel-bladed butcher and hunting knives, not to mention rifles and ammunition.

Sadly, the blessings were offset by deadly diseases—whooping cough, smallpox, measles, cholera, venereal infections, and, worst of all, alcoholism. Traders soon learned that Indians could easily be duped through the use of intoxicants, especially whiskey. Because liquor was new to Indians, they had not developed a tolerance for it over centuries of use, as whites had, and this led to the ruination of many Indians. For instance, in 1835, the exploring expedition of Colonel Henry Dodge visited a Cheyenne camp near Bent's Fort and

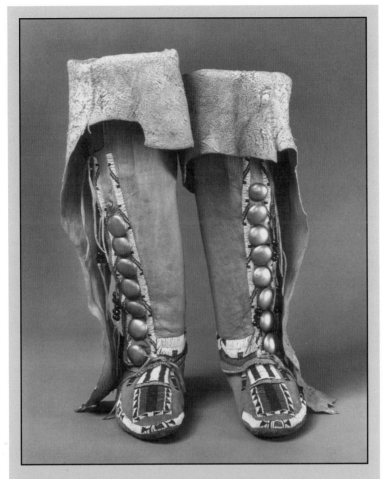

White traders often swapped beads and silver buttons, which are shown on these leggings, with the Cheyennes at Bent's Fort. In return, the Cheyennes provided robes and blankets to the white traders, who would then sell these goods in larger markets such as St. Louis, Missouri.

found the entire village besotted with whiskey. Men, women, and children dipped bowls and horn spoons into a large keg kept in the chief's lodge. The whiskey had been supplied by Mexican traders, who lured the inebriated Cheyennes into bartering away their robes, blankets, horses, and virtually all their personal belongings.

A thorough account of how whiskey ruined many

Cheyennes was supplied by Jim Beckwourth, a mulatto frontiersman who worked as a trader for the firm of Sublette and
Vasquez at its fort on the South Platte River in Colorado. In the
course of his dealings, he spent several years among the
Cheyennes, Arapahos, Crows, and Sioux. His adventures
became well known in 1856 with the publication of his autobi-
ography. In it, Beckwourth gave an excellent description of how
he and others used whiskey to swindle the Indians out of their
goods.

On one occasion, Beckwourth visited the camp of chiefs
Bob-tailed Horse and Old Bark. He brought two ten-gallon
kegs of whiskey, and within hours he had exchanged them for
buffalo robes. This was a tremendous bargain. A well-dressed
robe, the result of long and meticulous labor, fetched five dollars in St. Louis. In return, the Cheyennes accepted a pint of
whiskey, which cost the trader about six cents. As Beckwourth
put it:

> In two hundren gallons there are one thousand six hundrend
> pints [*hundren* and *hundrend* are old forms of *hundred*], for
> each one of which the trader gets a buffalo robe worth five
> dollars! The Indian women toil many long weeks to dress
> these one thousand six hundrend robes. The white trader
> gets them all for worse than nothing, for the poor Indian
> mother hides herself and her children in the forests until the
> effect of the poison passes away from the husbands, fathers,
> and brothers, who love them when they have no whiskey,
> and abuse and kill them when they have.

On another occasion, Beckwourth traded 4 kegs of
whiskey—some 60 gallons—for more than 1,100 robes and 18
horses, a total value of $6,000. Great as this margin of profit
was, it did not satisfy most traders. Many tipped the balance
more in their favor by diluting their whiskey with water to a
shameful extent, usually mixing in four gallons of water for
each gallon of alcohol. Others cheated by shorting the amount

of liquor they put in measuring cups or by inserting two fingers or a thumb into the cup as they poured. Some traders filled half the cup with tallow (animal fat).

Alcohol not only hurt the Cheyennes economically, it also damaged them morally. Rufus Sage, an 1841 visitor among the Sioux, Arapahos, and Cheyennes, witnessed scenes of drunken mayhem, as men, women, and children raced from tepee to tepee carrying vessels of liquor and whooping and singing drunkenly. A group of men quarreled and fought, while others staggered about in a daze or lay stretched helplessly on the ground.

Sometimes these episodes culminated in extreme violence and even murder. In November 1842, the American Fur Company sent several kegs of whiskey to a Cheyenne village on Chugwater Creek, a tributary of the North Platte River, in Wyoming. The alcohol, presented as a generous gift, was meant in fact to give the traders a leg up on competitors from rival companies. Its effect was tragic: The entire village became drunk and engaged in a brawl that left head chiefs Bull Bear and Yellow Lodge and six others dead.

Some chiefs recognized the danger of alcohol to the tribe's well-being. One such chief was Slim Face, a Southern Cheyenne who lived near Bent's Fort. In 1844, he resolved to confront U.S. government officials with the alcohol problem and also to inform them of the threat posed to the buffalo population by whites who were wantonly destroying the great herds. Slim Face joined a trading caravan headed for St. Louis, Missouri. His final destination was Washington, D.C., but he never made it there.

St. Louis overwhelmed Slim Face. He could not fathom how so many people could live in one village so far from the hunting grounds. He sat cross-legged on a St. Louis street corner and carved a notch in a stick each time a person passed by. Soon he had whittled the stick down to nothing. In dismay Slim Face realized he was dealing with an inexhaustible number of opponents. He gave up and returned home.

Slim Face's friend Old Wolf delighted in recounting an incident that occurred during the trip to St. Louis. At Independence, Missouri, a town along the way, Slim Face had boarded a steamboat for the first time. He was leaning against the rail that curved around the deck when the engineer's steam whistle suddenly sounded. Slim Face was so startled that he leaped into the river. He swam to safety and was given dry clothes. It was some time, however, before he could be persuaded to climb back on board. Old Wolf chided Slim Face for being frightened by something before he knew what it was.

Paying the Price

One of the few Cheyenne leaders to grasp the dangers of alcohol was Chief Porcupine Bear. His plea for abstinence, made to his brother-in-law Bobtailed Horse in the mid-nineteenth century is quoted in T.D. Bonner's *The Life and Adventures of James P. Beckwourth*, published in 1931:

Once we were a great and powerful nation: our hearts were proud and our arms were strong. But a few winters ago all other tribes feared us; now the Pawnees dare to cross our hunting grounds, and kill our buffalo. Once we could beat the Crows, and, unaided, destroyed their villages; now we call other villages to our assistance, and we can not defend ourselves from the assaults of the enemy. How is this, Cheyennes: The Crows drink no whiskey. The earnings of their hunters and toils of their women are bartered to the white man for weapons and ammunition. This keeps them powerful and dreaded by their enemies. We kill buffalo by the thousand; our women's hands are sore with dressing the robes; and what do we part with them to the white trader for? We pay them for the white man's firewater, which turns our brains upside down, which makes our hearts black, and renders our arms weak. It takes away our warriors' skill, and makes them shoot wrong in battle. Our enemies, who drink no whiskey, when they shoot, they always kill their foe. We have no ammunition to encounter our foes, and we have become as dogs, which have nothing but their teeth.

Slim Face retorted that if Old Wolf had been there, he would have jumped with him.

These years—the 1840s and 1850s—marked the final phase of largely friendly relations between the Cheyennes and whites. The problem of alcoholism aside, both groups often met on honorable terms, and time and again whites marveled at the innate nobility of the Plains Indian tribe and at the grandeur of their culture. There was little in the whites' experience that compared with the selflessness of the peace chiefs and the modesty of Cheyenne women. So impressed were

Our prairies were once covered with horses as the trees are covered with leaves. Where are they now? Ask the Crows, who drink no whiskey. When we are all drunk, they come and take them from before our eyes; our legs are helpless, and we can not follow them. We are only fearful to our women, who take up their children and conceal themselves among the rocks in the forest, for we are famishing. Our children are now sick, and our women are weak with watching. Let us not scare them away from our lodges, with their sick children in their arms. The Great Spirit will be offended at it. I had rather go to the great and happy hunting-ground now than live and see the downfall of my nation. Our fires begin to burn dim, and will soon go out entirely. My people are becoming like the Pawnees: they buy the whiskey of the trader, and, because he is weak and not able to fight them, they go and steal from his lodge.

I say, let us buy what is useful and good, but his whiskey we will not touch; let him take that away with him. I have spoke all I have to say, and if my brother wishes to kill me for it, I am ready to die. I will go and sit with my fathers in the spirit land, where I shall soon point down to the last expiring fire of the Cheyennes, and when they inquire the cause of this decline of their people, I will tell them with a straight tongue that it was the fire-water of the trader that put it out.

many of these visitors that they felt compelled to describe what they saw and thus unwittingly helped keep alive the memory of Cheyenne culture.

Sometimes the most casual encounters provided the most intriguing insights. For instance, in 1845, Colonel Stephen Watts Kearny led a detachment of men up the Platte River and met a band of Cheyennes on the Chugwater Creek. He found the encampment neat and "merry-looking." Hunters arrived with loads of buffalo meat. Women—in clothing decorated with shells, elk teeth, beads, and painted porcupine quills—sat about on buffalo robes. When one of Kearny's young officers peered closely at a Cheyenne girl to study her robe, she and her friends shrieked and giggled. They thought the officer's eyeglasses enabled him to see through the robes to the naked flesh underneath.

In 1845, Lieutenant J.W. Abert observed Cheyennes at Bent's Fort. He sketched Yellow Wolf and met his second chief, Old Bark, who voiced regret that he could not present Abert with a pictographed robe whose drawings showed his many exploits. Abert also met Old Bark's beautiful daughter, who was courted by many suitors. They tied horses to the door of her lodge to win her hand, but she would not give up her freedom.

Abert made a more serious discovery in that the Cheyennes were still at war with the Pawnees. Once, a large Cheyenne party galloped into Bent's Fort bearing a Pawnee scalp. Chief Little Crow and his relatives—their bodies blackened with ceremonial charcoal—led the Cheyennes inside the adobe fort to celebrate their success. They were joined by blanketed, trinketed women whose faces were daubed with red and black paint. The whole band performed a Scalp Dance accompanied by singing, by the beating of tambourines, and by war whoops. Abert, sketchbook in hand, observed the celebration and drew likenesses of the participants.

O-CUM-WHO-WAST.

U.S. Army Lieutenant J.W. Abert visited Bent's Fort in 1845 during his expedition to survey the area between New Mexico and St. Louis, Missouri, in preparation for the United States' planned annexation of Texas. While at Bent's Fort, Abert sketched many Cheyennes, including this young warrior.

Abert also witnessed a peace council that involved the Cheyennes and a group of Delaware Indians, who—having been driven from their territory in the East by white settlers— had become feared nomads in the West. In 1844, the Delawares lost fifteen men in an attack by a combined force of Cheyennes and Sioux. Old Bark worried that the Delawares would seek revenge. As a peace offering, he presented the Delawares with a fine horse. The Delawares responded by inviting the Cheyennes to join many other tribes in a grand council to be held at the Salt Plains in north-central Oklahoma. Both parties were satisfied and agreed to remain at peace.

Shortly after Abert's visit, two other white men stayed with the Cheyennes near the Arkansas River and gave useful accounts of what they saw. One, Englishman George Ruxton, spent time in a Cheyenne village at what the Indians called "Pretty Encampment," east of Bent's Fort. He described the camp's fifty or so tepees as arranged in rows of ten with the chief's tepee, dyed a conspicuous red, at the center. The homes of warriors and chiefs were decorated with paintings and symbols telling stories of warfare and heroic deeds. Spears and shields were stacked before each tepee, and in front of one stood a painted pole on which several smoke-dried scalps dangled. In Ruxton's words, they "rattled in the wind like a bag of peas."

Perhaps the most remarkable account of Cheyenne life was furnished in the 1840s by Lewis Garrard, a 17-year-old from Cincinnati, who traveled to the West for health reasons. Garrard joined a trading expedition returning to Bent's Fort by way of the Santa Fe Trail. He soon found himself deep inside the world of rough-hewn mountain men and nomadic Plains Indians. At the fort he was placed under the charge of John Simpson Smith, a trader married to a Cheyenne woman. With Smith, his wife and young son as his escort, Garrard took up residence in a Cheyenne camp.

He spent the winter of 1846–47 in Cheyenne camps along the Arkansas and described what he saw in *Wah-to-yah and the Taos Trail*, a classic of the early American frontier. During his two-month stay, Garrard enjoyed the hospitality of his hosts. With them he ate meals such as buffalo jerky and dried, pounded cherries mixed with buffalo marrow. More important, he observed the activities of the camp. Garrard watched Cheyenne men sit about a winter's lodge fire conversing and smoking *kinnikinnick* (ka-nick'-ku-nick'), a blend of tobacco, bark, dried leaves, herbs, and buffalo bone marrow. He was annoyed by the men who let the women do all of the work. He admired the Cheyenne father who held his young son in his arms and sang affectionate songs to him. He shivered in sympathy as a mother bathed her son and sent him outdoors naked for airing even on the coldest winter mornings. And he learned how the Cheyennes disciplined an unruly child by pouring icy water over his head until his energy was spent and his rage quenched.

The young adventurer from Ohio carefully studied the ways of the Cheyennes. He noted their love of games and gambling and their tribal dances, performed to the beat of drums and the unending "hay-a-hay, hay-a-hay" chanted in quickening tempo as prancing warriors brandished their shields, lances, and scalp trophies. He marveled at the vermilion-painted Cheyenne girls whose brass rings and bracelets glinted with the flickering light of the bonfire. He described the courtship procedure wherein a boy and girl wrapped themselves together in a blanket.

Other white observers charted the changing makeup of the Cheyenne tribe. From 1825 to 1850, the rift between the groups widened. Eventually the Cheyennes became segmented into three major geographical units. The Northern Cheyennes resided west of the Black Hills, a central group ranged along the South Platte, and the Southern Cheyennes remained on the Arkansas River.

Thaddeus A. Culbertson, who explored the upper Missouri River in 1850, stated that the Cheyennes, who numbered around three thousand people and three hundred lodges, were divided into three bands: the Dog Soldier band, the Half-breed band, and the Yellow Wolf band. There were other reports of "outlaw bands" of Cheyennes who had broken away from the main tribe and associated with neither the northern nor southern groups.

There was good reason that so many whites paid attention to the habits of the Cheyennes. The U.S. government had become increasingly aware of the need to establish better relations with the Indian nations of the West, to regulate trade, and to provide protection for its citizens who were streaming west in growing numbers, most of them headed for the rich farmland of the Midwest. Authorities wanted to extend American influence beyond the Mississippi River and to claim the land held by Mexico in the Southwest. As a result, more treaties were initiated, forts were built, and Indian agencies were established.

In 1846, the U.S. government appointed Thomas Fitzpatrick to serve as *agent* for the Cheyennes and Arapahos of the upper Arkansas River. Fitzpatrick had a great deal of experience with the western Indians and knew the Cheyennes from his days at the South Platte trading posts. His job was to cement good relations with the Indians and to conclude a new treaty defining their territory and securing their allegiance to the United States. Accordingly, the agent began arrangements for a great council of Plains Indians to be held in the vicinity of Fort Laramie on the North Platte.

The Treaty of Fort Laramie, signed on Horse Creek near the post in September 1851, was one of the spectacular events of the early West. It brought together the myriad tribal armies of the plains and mountains: Cheyennes, Arapahos, Assiniboines, Shoshones, Arikaras, Gros Ventres, Mandans, Sioux, Crows, Snakes, and representatives from smaller tribes. Hundreds of fully painted and feathered warriors arrived on horseback along with some ten thousand villagers whose tepees decorated the landscape.

This colorful spectacle included U.S. commissioners, who brought wagonloads of supplies and presents, escorted by blue-coated troops and accompanied by many renowned frontiersmen. One was Jim Bridger, who had personally escorted his Snake charges to the council. Another, John Simpson Smith, had lived eight years among the Blackfeet and more than twelve among the Cheyennes. He now served as official interpreter for the Cheyennes and Arapahos.

So diverse a gathering was bound to include longtime enemies. Indeed, shortly before the council convened, a Cheyenne war party had killed and scalped a Snake man and his son on the road to Salt Lake City. The Snake contingent demanded a settlement, and the Cheyennes agreed. An arbor made of lodge skins and poles was set up in a semicircle with one-half open on the east side. Skins and mats were arranged for seats. The Cheyenne chiefs, "as fine specimens of men as can be found anywhere," as a letter to the *Missouri Republican* noted, occupied half the seats, and the Snakes and the commissioners took the other.

The session began with a long period of silence, in which everyone present smoked from a pipe—a standard Indian protocol. Then Cheyenne chief Porcupine Bear rose and made a forceful speech. He urged his young men to accept the Snakes as friends, to take them by the hand, and to give them presents. He insisted that the young Cheyenne warriors should listen to the advice of the old men and not go to war without permission of the chiefs. Cheyenne elders urged the villagers to come forth.

A large copper kettle appeared, filled with boiled corn. From it a bowl was filled and passed around, each person serving himself with a ladle made from the horn of a black sheep. When the meal ended, Cheyenne chiefs made speeches exhorting their warriors to behave themselves and make peace with the Snakes. Following this, gifts were presented to the offended tribe. Each Cheyenne warrior rose to his feet, designated the recipient of his gift, and instructed his wife or child to deliver it. The recipient then embraced the bearer.

The council concluded when the Cheyennes who had killed the two Snakes returned their dried scalps. A grieving relative was consoled by assurances that the scalps had not been "danced" in celebration by the Cheyennes. He embraced the

After signing the Treaty of Fort Laramie with the U.S. government in 1851—which granted the Cheyennes land in northern Colorado—Cheyenne chiefs White Antelope (left) and Alights-on-the-Cloud (center), pictured here with Roman Nose, visited President Millard Fillmore in Washington, D.C. The Cheyenne delegates enjoyed their trip and were confident that a lasting peace had been established; unfortunately, the U.S. government quickly took back the land promised to the Cheyennes after a large number of white settlers streamed into the area during the Colorado Gold Rush, which began in 1859.

murderer, and a general whooping followed. A revelry of singing and dancing lasted through the night.

In their talks with the commissioners, the Cheyennes delegated Wan-es-sah-ta, or He Who Walks with His Toes Turned Out, to speak for them. He met with U.S. Indian superintendent D.D. Mitchell, who offered to repay the tribes for their loss of buffalo range and grassland. The treaty drawn up for the Cheyennes and Arapahos defined boundaries for their territory. Its northern and southern borders were rivers: to the north, the North Platte, which flows from Wyoming into Nebraska; to the south, the Arkansas, which runs through the lower half of Kansas, Oklahoma, and Arkansas. Its eastern border was a line through western Kansas; its western border was the Rocky Mountains. The tribes agreed to allow the United States to build roads and military posts within their territory and to recognize U.S. sovereignty.

While all the assembled Indians feasted, hosted one another, and deliberated on the proposed treaty, a group of Cheyenne warriors, stripped of clothing and painted for war, presented an exhibition of horsemanship and battle maneuvers, making mock charges upon enemies with guns, lances, and bows. The display concluded with a war dance during which Cheyenne braves recounted their heroic deeds against foes.

The treaty was signed on September 17, 1851. The commission then determined that a delegation composed of representatives from all the Indian tribes should visit President Millard Fillmore in Washington, D.C. Three Cheyenne delegates were chosen: Little Chief, White Antelope, and Alights-on-the-Cloud. En route the party paused in Kansas to hold a peace council with the Pawnees before moving on to St. Louis, where they boarded a steamboat.

The Indians shrank from boarding the smoke-belching "fire horse," but soon their fears subsided, and they were delighted with the ride. In Washington, D.C., they met with President Fillmore at the White House and were taken on tours of the city. They visited local forts, naval yards, and arsenals. They were most amazed by the Central Market and its domestic fowl hanging in rows. The Indians enjoyed the trip so much that they did not return to their homes until January 1852. They arrived at their camps filled with hope for the future.

5

Massacre on Sand Creek

Like so many of the treaties Indians signed with the U.S. government, the agreement devised at Fort Laramie created more
confusion than harmony. The Indians who signed it had no
inkling that their land would subsequently be invaded. Nor did
they imagine that white settlers would pour into their land in
large numbers. In 1853 alone—two years after the treaty was
signed—fifteen thousand whites passed through Fort Laramie on
Nebraska's Platte Trail. These intruders not only killed a great deal
of game, they also brought diseases and often abused the Indians
they encountered.

Similar problems developed on the Santa Fe Trail, the great
transportation route along the Arkansas River. As whites flocked
west, conflicts developed between them and the Indians. The first
serious conflict between the Cheyennes and the U.S. Army occurred
in April 1856 at a bridge on the upper Platte River near what is now

Laramie, Wyoming. A military officer attempted to arrest three Cheyennes for the theft of a horse. When the Cheyennes attempted to flee, one of them was killed.

Not long after this, an old trapper in the Black Hills was murdered by two Cheyennes. In June 1856, a party of Cheyennes and Arapahos attacked a pioneer wagon train on the Platte Trail, and in August some Cheyenne youths harassed and wounded a mail-wagon driver near Fort Kearny, Nebraska. Troops from the fort responded with an attack on a Cheyenne camp, killing ten people and wounding several more. It was inevitable that war erupt as infuriated Cheyenne warriors repeatedly attacked settlers. U.S. Army officers grew convinced that retaliation was necessary. In the summer of 1857, the first major military operation against the Cheyennes was undertaken, commanded by Colonel E.V. "Bull of the Woods" Sumner, a white-bearded, deep-voiced officer with a reputation as a ferocious fighter.

In July, Sumner confronted a large force of Cheyenne warriors on the Republican River, which flows through southern Nebraska and Kansas. Sumner attacked with an unexpected saber charge, driving the Indians from the field. Cheyenne dead numbered between twenty and thirty, but Sumner's casualties were minimal: two men killed and nine wounded. Thus, though their loss of warriors was not great, the Cheyennes had suffered a setback in their first major confrontation with the U.S. Army.

Further conflict arose during the Colorado Gold Rush, which peaked in the fall of 1859. At that time, William Bent was appointed by the U.S. government to act as Indian agent for the Cheyennes and Arapahos. Both these tribes were divided by the South Platte, half of each group living south of the river and half to the north. In December 1859, Bent reported to the superintendent of Indian affairs in St. Louis that both tribes were uneasy. They resented the invasion of gold prospectors and settlers who built such towns as Denver on their choicest land.

Despite this intrusion and their displeasure with the traffic that was spoiling their hunting grounds, the Cheyennes and Arapahos continued to abide by the terms of the Treaty of Fort Laramie.

In 1859, the Northern Cheyennes, along with the Sioux and Northern Arapahos, signed a treaty with Thomas S. Twiss of the North Platte Agency. The Northern Cheyennes joined the other tribes in ceding a vast area of land in present-day western Kansas, Nebraska, and the Dakotas. In return, the Cheyennes received a reservation on the Laramie River of southeastern Wyoming and were awarded a yearly payment, or annuity, of $16,000.

Meanwhile, the Southern Cheyennes and Arapahos, both destitute, petitioned the U.S. government for the region in Colorado between the Arkansas River and the Raton Mountains. According to Bent, they also requested assistance in building homes and learning to raise crops. Arrangements were made to hold another treaty council with the southern bands.

On September 8, 1860, the federal commissioner of Indian Affairs, A.B. Greenwood, arrived at Bent's New Fort (erected in 1853 near Lamar, in the southeastern tip of Colorado, near the Kansas border). He brought thirteen wagonloads of trinkets and goods, and initiated a new treaty that called for the Cheyennes to settle on a reservation just to the north of the Arkansas River. It was signed by chiefs Black Kettle, White Antelope, Lean Bear, Little Wolf, Tall Bear, and Left Hand. Cheyenne and Arapaho tribesmen, however, objected to being confined to an arid reservation unfit either for farming or hunting. The federal government promised them food, clothing, and other goods, but the tribes preferred their traditional way of life, which revolved around the buffalo.

The Indians' objections were justified. The extremely dry summer of 1861 was very hard on the southern bands. In

A delegation of southern Plains Indian chiefs, including representatives of the Cheyennes, met with President Abraham Lincoln in March 1863. The group, which included War Bonnet, Standing in the Water, and Lean Bear (all shown here in the front row, left to right), promised the president that the Cheyennes would not break the treaties they signed with the U.S. government.

September, they gathered at Fort Wise—located in Colorado, near Bent's Fort—and demanded the annuities promised them under the past treaties. The post commander had few supplies himself, but he distributed enough to quiet the threats being made against the fort.

Even as tensions mounted during this period, the Southern Cheyennes and Arapahos remained peaceful. Other tribes showed less restraint. The Comanches and Kiowas launched repeated raids on wagon trains traveling along the Santa Fe Trail. By spring 1863, the situation had become explosive, and newly appointed Indian agent Samuel G. Colley led a delegation of Indian chiefs to Washington, D.C. The Cheyennes sent Lean Bear, War Bonnet, and Standing in the Water to represent them.

Lean Bear spoke for the group in a meeting with President Abraham Lincoln in the East Room of the White House. John Simpson Smith interpreted for Lean Bear, who assured Lincoln the chiefs would take his advice seriously. Lean Bear explained that he longed to keep peace on the plains but that many white men preferred war. Lincoln replied that the U.S. government shared Lean Bear's desire for peace, and he promised every effort would be made to uphold it, even if some whites violated treaty agreements. But, he observed, "It is not always possible for any father to have his children do precisely as he wishes them to do." Despite this warning, the Indian chiefs departed satisfied that Lincoln had communicated the goodwill of his nation.

Nonetheless, hostilities flared during the summer of 1863. A Cheyenne was shot and killed by a guard at Fort Larned in western Kansas, and rumors that Indians there planned a "war of extermination" against whites spread through Colorado. In response, territorial governor John Evans dispatched a frontiersman to contact the tribes and invite their chiefs to a peace council. But the chiefs, on a buffalo hunt in the Smoky Hill area of western Kansas, claimed they were needed by their people, many of whom were dying of whooping cough and dysentery. In addition, their horses could not manage so long a trip.

The crisis grew when some Northern Arapahos killed a family of white settlers in Denver and nearly touched off a panic. Colonel John M. Chivington, who commanded the military district of Colorado, seized on the incident as an excuse to send troops to the South Platte with instructions to "be sure you have the right ones, and then kill them." The Colorado First Cavalry attacked several Cheyenne camps in northern Colorado. More damage also resulted from the campaign of Lieutenant George S. Eayre, who led troops from Denver into western Kansas. They followed the Republican River, intent on finding and killing Indians. On May 16, 1864, they encountered a group of Cheyennes who were on a large buffalo hunt north of Fort Larned.

The hunt was headed by Chief Lean Bear, just back from his meeting with President Lincoln. When the chief spotted the approaching troops, he and another Cheyenne rode forward to meet them. On his chest Lean Bear bore the large peace medal given to him in Washington, D.C., and carried a note signed by the president testifying that the chief could be trusted. It proved of no avail. As soon as the two Indians came within range, the soldiers opened fire and killed both. Eayre then scurried to the safety of Fort Larned. This episode pushed the tribes over the edge during the summer of 1864. Kansas paid the price, as Cheyenne warriors, led by the Dog Soldier band, struck with fury at wagon trains and outlying settlements.

Governor Evans issued a proclamation directing friendly Cheyennes to appear at the various U.S. government forts. In response, Black Kettle and the other Cheyenne leaders sent a message to Fort Lyon. It was written by One Eye, whose daughter was married to a white man living near the Arkansas River. The commander of Fort Lyon, Major Edward W. Wynkoop, moved by the sincerity of the Cheyennes, led an expedition to Smoky Hill, where he conducted an interview with the chiefs.

Wynkoop again was impressed by the intelligence, understanding, and candor of Chief Black Kettle. The chief, wrote Wynkoop in his memoirs, sat "calm, dignified, immovable with a slight smile on his face." Wynkoop inspired equal trust in Black Kettle. This mutual respect helped Wynkoop persuade the Cheyennes to send a delegation to Denver to meet with Governor Evans. Black Kettle made the journey, along with White Antelope and Bull Bear, a brother of Lean Bear and the leader of the Dog Soldiers.

At Denver's Camp Weld, Black Kettle made a brief but eloquent speech. He said, as the secretary of war reported to Congress, "We have come with our eyes shut, following [Wynkoop's] handful of men, like coming through the fire. All we ask is that we may have peace with the whites. You are our father; we have been travelling through a cloud; the sky has been dark ever since the war began." At this time, both Evans and Chivington were running for political office in Colorado, and their campaign tactics included pandering to the voters' anti-Indian bias. Evans openly accused the Cheyenne chiefs of initiating hostilities. Chivington did not comment until the end of the conference, when he stated: "My rule of fighting white men or Indians is, to fight them until they lay down their arms and submit to military authority. You are nearer Major Wynkoop than any one else, and you can go to him when you get ready to do that."

Chivington's remarks implied that if the Indians came to Fort Lyon, they would be safe. The chiefs returned to their bands and persuaded them to take that risk in order to secure peace. In November, nine Cheyennes arrived at Fort Lyon and reported that some six hundred of their people were on their way and that two thousand more would follow once the weather improved.

In the interim, Wynkoop, whose superiors thought him too "soft" on Indians, was relieved of his command at Fort Lyon. His replacement was Major Scott J. Anthony. By the time Anthony took command, some 113 lodges of Arapahos—a total of 652 people—had already arrived at Fort Lyon. They were destitute, but Anthony had no food to give them. He dispatched John Smith with instructions that the smaller group of Cheyennes, Black Kettle's band, should remain in their camp at the bend of Sand Creek, north of the fort. Anthony promised they would be safe, and Black Kettle complied.

Meanwhile, other plans were under way in Denver. In August, Governor Evans secured the authority to recruit a new regiment of volunteer cavalry, the Colorado Third, whose enlistments lasted one hundred days. Little use was made of the regiment, and in Denver it became known, mockingly, as the "Bloodless Third." The regiment was nearing the end of its one-hundred-day enlistment without having fought a single battle. Feeling the pressure of political embarrassment and threatened

In late November 1864, a group of Arapahos and Southern Cheyennes had set up camp along the banks of Big Sandy Creek in southeastern Colorado. On the morning of November 29, U.S. Army Colonel John Chivington led the Colorado Third Volunteer Cavalry into the camp, where they attacked the unsuspecting Arapahos and Cheyennes, who believed that they were under the protection of the U.S. government. More than 150 Arapahos and Cheyennes were killed, most of whom were women and children.

by the recent arrival in Denver of General P.E. Connor, Chivington ordered the volunteer regiment to begin a march to Sand Creek in southeastern Colorado. He stopped at Fort Lyon and added its garrison to his forces.

Chivington now headed seven hundred troops, all armed with short-barreled carbines and pistols. His command also included four twelve-pound mountain howitzers, or cannons. The cavalry marched steadily northward in columns of four until, under a bright, starlit sky, it reached the Cheyenne encampment.

Dawn had barely broken when the troops spied the snaking

tree line of Sand Creek (also known as Big Sandy Creek). They next saw the tepees of Black Kettle's village, which was nestled comfortably in the crook of a large bend of Sand Creek. A range

Account of the Sand Creek Massacre

The Sand Creek Massacre still haunts the Cheyenne people. On November 29, 1864, regiments of the Colorado state militia led by Colonel John Chivington attacked a peaceful encampment of Cheyennes and Arapahos, who had followed instructions by federal authorities to settle near Fort Lyon. The state militia attacked the encampment anyway, killing more than 150 Cheyennes and Arapahos, most of them women, children, and infants. Congressional investigations determined that the attack was a massacre and not a legitimate military operation, but no Colorado soldiers were ever punished. Little Bear, an eyewitness to the attack, later relayed his experiences at Sand Creek to George Bent, a mixed-blooded Cheyenne:

> The [Cheyenne and Arapaho] people were all running up the creek; the soldiers sat on their horses, lined up on the banks and firing into the camps, but they soon saw the lodges were now nearly empty, so they began to advance up the creek, firing on the fleeing people. . . . After leaving the others, I started to run up the creek bed in the direction taken by most of the fleeing people, but I had not gone far when a party of about twenty cavalrymen got into the dry bed of the stream behind me. They chased me up the creek for about two miles, very close behind me and firing on me all the time. Nearly all the feathers were shot out of my war bonnet, and some balls passed through my shield; but I was not touched. I passed many women and children, dead and dying, lying in the creek bed. The soldiers had not scalped them yet, as they were busy chasing those that were yet alive. After the fight I came back down the creek and saw these dead bodies all cut up, and even the wounded scalped and slashed. . . . I ran up the creek about two miles and came to the place where a large party of people had taken refuge in holes dug in the sand up against the sides of the high banks. I stayed here until the soldiers withdrew. They were on both banks, firing down upon us, but not many of us were killed. All who failed to reach these pits in the sand were shot down.

of sand hills loomed above the south bank of the bend. Beyond the village, the north bank fell away on a gradual plane, defined on the west by the course of the creek. Camp dogs barked, and the troops knew they had been seen. Without pausing, Chivington immediately ordered his five battalions into action. One drove between the village and a huge horse herd grazing in the meadows to the east. Another set off to capture the herd on the back side of the bluffs south and west of the encampment.

Startled Cheyennes stumbled out of their lodges as the other Colorado units dismounted and rained rifle and pistol fire into the melee. They set up howitzers that lobbed clusters of grapeshot—small iron balls and canisters of lead and iron— into the hide-covered tepees. Among those in the camp were John Simpson Smith and the two half-Indian sons of William Bent, George and Charlie.

Cheyenne warriors fought desperately to stem the advance of the troops, and women fled with their children into the bed of Sand Creek. Black Kettle raised an American flag in order to show that his camp was friendly. The action was futile. White Antelope walked forward toward his attackers with his hands held high, imploring them not to shoot. Finally he stopped in the middle of the creek bed with his arms folded and was killed. Once the camp was routed, the troops pursued the fleeing figures, shooting or hacking them down with sabers. A group of women and children tried to hide in a cut in the river bank, but they were discovered by soldiers who had great sport picking off their victims one by one.

By 3:00 P.M. the shooting had ceased, and the troops began looting the village. Some of the one-hundred-day volunteers took scalps. John Simpson Smith escaped harm, but his half-Indian son Jack was captured and murdered; his corpse was harnessed to a horse and dragged around the campsite. Black Kettle and his wife managed to escape. The bodies on the battlefield included those of One Eye and Arapaho chief Left Hand.

In his report, Chivington claimed that four hundred to five

hundred Indians had been killed, compared with a loss to his own forces of nine killed and thirty-eight wounded. He tried to glorify the Sand Creek Massacre by referring to it not as a slaughter but as "one of the most bloody Indian battles ever fought on these plains."

Cheyenne women made leggings from the hides of buffalo, which they often adorned with beads obtained from white traders. These women's leggings, which are decorated with German silver conchas and yellow, white, red, and blue Italian beads, are housed at the Colorado Historical Society in Denver, Colorado. On the right is a pouch, which is decorated with beadwork.

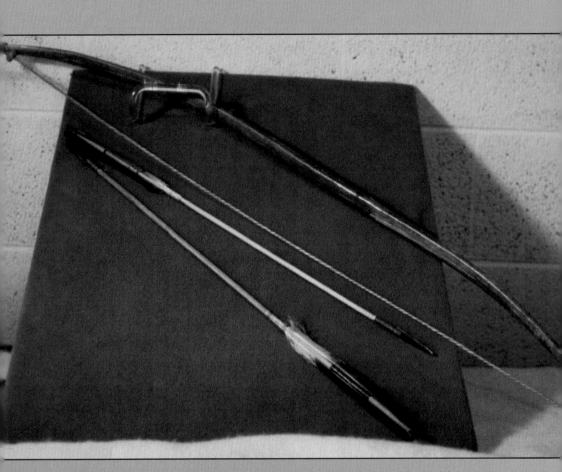

After the Cheyennes obtained horses, they no longer had to drive the buffalo over cliffs or into an area where they could easily surround and kill them. Instead, they were able to ride among the buffalo and kill them with arrows shot from bows. Shown here are two Cheyenne arrows, made from willow and alder trees, and a wooden bow that was found at Sand Creek, Colorado.

This Northern Cheyenne war bonnet, which is on display at the Colorado Historical Society, was worn by Chief Wooden Leg, a participant in the Battle of the Little Bighorn.

This leather tinder pouch, which is adorned with beadwork, is from the Tongue River Reservation in Montana. Tinder pouches were used prior to the invention of matches and lighters to help light pipes or fires.

When Cheyenne warriors headed into battle, they often carried bows, arrows, lances, battle-axes, and shields, such as this one which is brandished with bright feathers and made of buffalo hide.

Eagle-bone whistles are often used in such sacred Cheyenne ceremonies as the Sun Dance, which is held every summer and symbolically celebrates the renewal of the world.

Modeled after a tepee used by a member of the Elk society—one of five Cheyenne military societies—this reproduction is made from buckskin and is housed at the Field Museum of Natural History in Chicago.

Cheyenne men and women both wore moccasins, which had rawhide soles and were adorned with beads. This pair is on display at the National Museum of Natural History in Washington, D.C.

6

Losing Battles

As Black Kettle and his band of elders, women, and children fled south of the Arkansas River, Cheyenne drums summoned warriors to the headwaters of the Republican River. Chivington's betrayal and massacre of the peaceful band of Southern Cheyennes at Sand Creek had catapulted the military societies, particularly the Dog Soldiers, to great power within the tribe, and at the meeting, furious war leaders exhorted some two thousand Cheyenne, Arapaho, and Sioux fighters to "make war to the knife" against the whites.

From camps in Kansas and Colorado, the Cheyennes mounted assaults against travelers and frontier settlements. In January 1865, they staged a well-organized strike on Fort Rankin on the South Platte Trail near the small settlement of Julesburg, Colorado. First a war party attacked a wagon train near the fort, killing twelve men. Next, the Cheyennes drew a company out of the fort and massacred every man. Then they overran the defenseless settlement, burning

Many Southern Cheyenne chiefs, including Bull Bear, refused to settle on the Darlington Agency, the reservation set up for the tribe by the U.S. government in 1867. Over the next eight years, bands of Southern Cheyennes continued to elude the U.S. Army, but by 1875 they were on the brink of starvation and were forced to surrender.

buildings, looting, and making off with as much plunder as their horses could carry.

Many Southern Cheyenne bands moved northward to the protection of the Black Hills, and—as they crossed the Platte— fought an indecisive battle with troops from Fort Laramie, Wyoming. In April 1865, Cheyennes were said to have visited the Sioux north of the Black Hills and to have incited them to join their war against the U.S. Army. Meanwhile, sporadic attacks against settlers continued along both the Platte and Arkansas trails. Sometimes they were carried out by the Cheyennes and Arapahos, sometimes by the Comanches and Kiowas. Both groups raided wagon trains, stole horses, killed and scalped civilians, plundered stagecoach stations, and destroyed telegraph lines.

The U.S. government was divided in its response. The army prepared for a punitive campaign against the Indians in western Kansas, but Comanche-Kiowa agent Jesse Leavenworth pushed for a new peace council and new treaties. He sent Jesse Chisholm, a frontiersman and trader, on a trip southward into Indian Territory to persuade the Comanches and the Kiowas to participate. Intermediaries also contacted Black Kettle, then camped on Wolf Creek in northwestern Oklahoma. Despite threats by the Dog Soldiers that their horses would be killed, Black Kettle, George Bent, and their families attended a council held at the mouth of the Little Arkansas River (the site of what is now Wichita, Kansas). There, in early August, the Indians agreed to appear at yet another peace council, this time in October.

The council included a wide range of famous men of the frontier, representing both Indian nations and the federal government. Frontiersmen such as Kit Carson and William Bent attended, as did James Steele, who represented the *Bureau of Indian Affairs* (BIA), the federal agency founded in 1824 and recognized by Congress ten years later. Also present were Leavenworth, Chisholm, John Simpson Smith, and many other Western notables.

In his opening speech to the commission, Black Kettle stated the grievances of Indians who desired peace. "Your young soldiers—I don't think they listen to you," he said. "You bring presents, and when I come to get them I am afraid they will strike me before I get away. When I come in to receive presents I take them up crying. Although wrongs have been done me I live in hopes. I have not got two hearts." Then he added: "My shame is as big as the earth. . . . I once thought that I was the only man that persevered to be the friend of the white man, but since they have come and [robbed] our lodges, horses and everything else, it is hard for me to believe white men any more."

The Treaty of the Little Arkansas granted the Cheyennes and Arapahos a new reservation area on the Cimarron River. In exchange, they gave up their last tribal claim to lands in Colorado. Black Kettle and a few other Cheyenne and Arapaho chiefs signed the treaty, but they represented only a small portion of the southern bands. The Dog Soldiers and other warrior groups had no intention of giving up their buffalo hunting grounds in western Kansas. During the winter of 1865–66, Cheyenne warrior bands killed and scalped several people, burned stagecoach and railroad stations, and harassed transport wagons.

Major General Winfield Scott Hancock, newly assigned as military commander in Kansas, threatened a retaliatory war if the Cheyennes did not surrender to him those guilty of the crimes committed along the Smoky Hill River in Kansas. In March 1867, Hancock departed Fort Riley, Kansas, with 1,400 infantry, artillery, cavalry, scouts, wagon drivers, and others, who all marched to Fort Larned. Hancock's subordinate, Lieutenant Colonel George Armstrong Custer, commanded the U.S. Seventh Cavalry.

After a brief delay caused by a late-spring blizzard, a meeting with the chiefs of a large village of Cheyennes and Sioux was arranged by Wynkoop, who had become an Indian agent. Hancock exercised little diplomacy. He curtly told the Indians that if they did not behave at the meeting they would be killed. He then ordered his army to advance toward the Indian camp. They were met by a large force of Cheyennes and Sioux drawn up in a battle line. Violence was averted when Wynkoop rode forward with a white truce flag. When Hancock entered the camp the next morning, he was enraged to learn that during the night the Indians, fearing another Sand Creek, had fled, leaving their tepees behind.

Hancock ordered Custer to pursue them. He did so, following a confusing trail that frequently forked off to both the left and the right. Custer doggedly hewed to the middle course until finally it faded away into the prairie of western Kansas. Meanwhile, Hancock burned the tepees and equipage of the village, an act that further fueled the anger and distrust of the Cheyennes.

During the summer, Plains Indians committed more raids on Smoky Hill, so Custer led another campaign through the barren country of northwestern Kansas. Again his efforts proved futile. He met the enemy only once, and his troops were outmaneuvered by a Sioux party under Pawnee Killer. The Sioux chief was believed to be responsible later for the deaths of Lieutenant Lyman Kidder, ten cavalrymen, and a Sioux scout whose mutilated corpses were discovered by Custer's troops.

For their part, the Cheyennes continued to hamper American expansion and commerce in the plains. Authorities debated over how best to deal with them. White settlers in Kansas joined the U.S. Army in demanding a punitive war, whereas Indian Bureau "olive branchers" urged another peace effort. The U.S. government chose this second approach, and Congress voted funds for a peace commission to draw up another treaty with the southern Plains tribes.

This time Leavenworth himself journeyed to the Salt Fork of the Arkansas, in northern Oklahoma, to persuade the Comanches and Kiowas to attend still another treaty council in 1867. Other couriers traveled to the camps of the Cheyennes and Arapahos on Wolf Creek. Finally, it was arranged for a grand council to be held that autumn on Medicine Lodge Creek in the extreme south of Kansas.

The meeting began with the tribes involved—the Cheyenne, Arapaho, Comanche, Kiowa, and Plains Apache—all airing their

grievances. Presents were then distributed by the peace commission, which had no difficulty signing new agreements with
each tribe, except the Cheyenne. Black Kettle and his peace fac-
tion willingly granted new concessions, but the stubborn Dog
Soldiers refused to join the proceedings. Instead, they made the
commission wait while they conducted their rite of Renewal of
the Medicine Arrows.

When they finally arrived, the Dog Soldiers showed open
disdain for the council, but eventually they were persuaded to
sign the treaty. It relegated them to a reservation area along the
Salt Fork of the Arkansas River in Indian Territory (now
Oklahoma). The band agreed to go there only after a member
of the commission made an unofficial spoken commitment
that contradicted the written terms of the treaty by saying that
the Cheyennes would be permitted to hunt buffalo north of the
Arkansas River. This false assurance on a key issue would ultimately doom the Treaty of Medicine Lodge Creek.

Even if the treaty's contradictions had been cleared up,
problems between the Cheyennes and whites would have persisted. Westward expansion had become a rallying cry for the
U.S. government, and the stubborn presence of the Cheyennes
in western Kansas alarmed settlers who were pushing into their
country. Anti-Indian sentiment in the state peaked when a war
party consisting of Cheyennes, Arapahos, and Sioux made a
raid upon some Kansas settlements. The warriors had intended
to raid a Pawnee village, but instead they had gotten drunk and
attacked frontier outposts along the Saline and Solomon rivers.
They committed murder and rape and carried off captives.

Demands for retaliation rang out loudly through the territory. In response, General Philip H. Sheridan, the military commander in Kansas, authorized the formation of a special unit of
white frontiersmen under Colonel George A. Forsyth. Sheridan
reasoned that a small team of scouts, unencumbered by the
heavy equipment of a larger military force, would have better
luck ferreting out the Indians. Forsyth plunged into Cheyenne

territory west of Fort Wallace. He was accompanied by approximately fifty mounted scouts, who discovered signs of Indian presence as they proceeded up the Republican River. After heading into camp on the evening of September 16, the party saw an Indian signal fire on a distant hill.

The following dawn, while the scouts' coffeepots still sat on the fire, the Cheyennes struck. Several warriors rushed at the troops' horses, waving blankets and war whooping. Hundreds more appeared from all directions, sounding their battle cry and firing as they surged forward. The scouts fled to a sandbar on the river and were pinned down there. They held off numerous charges, some led by the great Cheyenne warrior Roman Nose. His appearance commanded attention as he guided his men down the riverbed against the sandbar fortification, his beautiful, feathered headdress trailing behind. During one such assault, however, a bullet from a scout ended his life.

For nine days the scouts were besieged and held to the sandbar, enduring sniper fire, severe hunger, and the stench of their dead horses. Several of their party perished, including surgeon John Mooers and Lieutenant Fred Beecher, nephew of the noted New York preacher Henry Ward Beecher. Forsyth himself was badly wounded at the onset of the fight but survived until a rescue column arrived on September 25. At the same time that these Cheyennes quashed Forsyth's forces, the bands who had taken refuge below the Arkansas River repulsed an inept venture into northwestern Indian Territory by General Alfred Sully.

These botched military efforts convinced Sheridan that catching and defeating the fleet-ponied Plains Indian warriors on the open prairie was next to impossible. He concluded that it would be necessary to strike the Cheyennes in their home camps with a winter's campaign.

Other elements of the U.S. government were still trying to work out amicable relations with the Cheyennes. Even as Sheridan was formulating his plans, the U.S. government reestablished previously abandoned Fort Cobb in Oklahoma as an Indian agency. It was now to become an Indian sanctuary. General William B. Hazen was appointed to supervise the issuance of goods and supplies to peaceful tribes seeking refuge there.

As winter approached, the Cheyennes under Black Kettle and Little Robe withdrew even deeper to the south, camping in western Oklahoma near the Antelope Hills, where they joined Arapahos, Comanches, Kiowas, and Plains Apaches. On November 20, Black Kettle led a party of Cheyennes and Arapahos to Fort Cobb for talks with Hazen. He told the officer that his band of 180 lodges, then encamped on the Washita River, wished for peace and were willing to move to Fort Cobb. Hazen rejected the plea. He stated that he lacked the authority to make peace and warned the chiefs that Sheridan's troops were coming to fight them. The chiefs returned to their camps. Black Kettle's band of fifty tepees was now the farthest west of the winter camps of some six thousand other Indians.

On the night of November 26, Black Kettle convened a meeting of his band's elders at his lodge to discuss their situation. They had been denied access to Fort Cobb, Sheridan was on their trail, and they needed to decide on a plan of action. One man told of a big troop contingent seen by a Kiowa war party in the snow, north of the Canadian River. Some scoffed at the idea that "blue-coats" would be out in such cold weather. Others felt they were far enough south to be safe from attack. They all agreed, however, that they should move their camp downriver the following day.

The danger was much greater than the Cheyenne elders realized. Sheridan had planned a three-pronged winter campaign into Oklahoma. His main force, camped at Fort Dodge, Kansas, would be joined by forces sent down from Fort Lyon, Colorado, and from Fort Bascom, New Mexico, in the west. The main command had already reached the juncture of Beaver and Wolf creeks on November 18 and set about erecting temporary quarters named Camp Supply.

In late November 1868, nearly four years to the day after the Sand Creek Massacre, U.S. Lieutenant Colonel George Armstrong Custer attacked a Cheyenne village on the banks of the Washita River in Oklahoma. Among the casualties was Chief Black Kettle, whose death was devastating to the Cheyennes. Shown here is the monument that recognizes the two main combatants in the battle. Washita Battlefield was designated a National Historic Site in 1996.

Five days later, in a howling snowstorm, the Seventh Cavalry, led by Custer, marched southwest down Wolf Creek in search of Indians. After turning south to the Antelope Hills, a scouting party discovered an Indian trail heading across the snow-covered prairie toward the Washita River. Leaving his wagons and making a forced march throughout the starlit night of November 26, 1868, Custer located and surrounded an Indian village nestled in a bend of the Washita.

It was Black Kettle's band—the remnants of the same band that had been massacred at Sand Creek by Chivington. On November 27, 1868—almost four years to the day after Sand Creek—Custer attacked at dawn. Just as they had four years earlier, the Cheyennes awoke to the sounds of bugles, gunfire, and whooping cavalrymen charging pell-mell into their village. Once again the slaughter was merciless. Indian men, women, and children were cut down by bullets and sabers as they fled for their lives. Among them were the great peacemaker Black Kettle and his wife, both killed as they attempted to wade across the Washita on a single horse.

After burning the Cheyennes' lodges, robes, clothing, food, and saddles and shooting their horses, Custer found himself surrounded by warriors from the villages downriver. In a letter to the *New York Times*, Frederick Benteen described them as "savages on flying steeds, with shields and feathers gay . . . circling everywhere, riding like devils incarnate." During the battle, an informal detachment under Major Joel Elliott had disappeared in pursuit of Cheyennes. They had not been seen since. With Indians swarming the hills above him, Custer realized he was cut off from the supply train he had left behind at the Antelope Hills. He regrouped his forces and feigned a march farther downstream toward the Indian camps. Then, under cover of darkness, he turned about and retreated to Camp Supply, taking as captives several Cheyenne women and children.

Days later, Sheridan led his army back to the battlefield where the corpses of missing troops were found along with the bodies of civilians captured previously on the Santa Fe Trail. Sheridan then proceeded to Fort Cobb and set up headquarters while his other forces—from New Mexico and Colorado—scoured the Texas panhandle for Indians.

In January 1869, Sheridan established a new military post in Oklahoma, at Fort Sill, near the Wichita Mountains on Medicine Bluff Creek. Custer and his Seventh Cavalry, which had been joined at Camp Supply by the Nineteenth Kansas Volunteer Cavalry Regiment, remained at this fort until March 2. On his return march to Kansas, Custer took a circuitous route into the Texas panhandle in an attempt to rescue two white women who were known to be held captive by the Cheyennes.

After a grueling march, Custer's scouts finally found an Indian trail that led them to a Cheyenne camp on the Sweetwater Creek, just west of the 100th meridian, the line that marks the boundary between Oklahoma and the Texas panhandle. Custer, his forces badly worn out and in disarray, received a friendly greeting from Cheyenne chief Medicine Arrows. Through Mo-na-se-tah, an Indian girl whom he had taken captive on the Washita, Custer learned that the two white women, taken in Kansas during the previous summer, were being held in the Cheyenne camp.

Custer lured the Cheyenne chiefs to his camp and then took three of them hostage. He threatened to hang them if the two women were not released. Eventually Anna Morgan and Sarah White, wearing only flour sacks, were brought in. Custer, however, reneged on his promise to release the three Cheyenne captives. Instead, he took them with him as he and his command marched back to Kansas via Camp Supply, leaving the southern bands of the Cheyennes scattered upon the prairie, severely weakened. However, the fighting spirit of the Cheyenne warrior societies was far from dead.

At the same time that chiefs Little Robe, Minimic, and others met with Colonel Benjamin Grierson at Fort Sill and agreed to settle on a reservation in the Camp Supply vicinity, 165 tepees of Dog Soldiers, led by Tall Bull and White Horse, headed north to join the Sioux on the Republican River in western Kansas. There they were attacked by troops under the command of Major E.A. Carr. The Cheyennes put up a stout resistance before fleeing, leaving twenty-five dead warriors on the field.

Once again the Dog Soldiers launched retaliatory raids against settlements, wagon transports, and outposts of the Kansas Pacific Railroad, each time taking prisoners. Carr followed in pursuit. In July 1869, guided by Pawnee scouts under the command of Frank and Luther North, he located Tall Bull's

After the U.S. Seventh Cavalry killed at least one hundred Cheyennes, including Chief Black Kettle, at the Battle of the Washita on November 29, 1868, Lieutenant Colonel George Armstrong Custer (pictured here) continued to lead a punitive campaign against the Cheyennes in the spring of 1869. Custer believed that by arresting several chiefs at a Cheyenne village on Sweetwater Creek in the Texas panhandle in March 1869, he would be able to convince all Southern Cheyennes to surrender.

village north of the Platte River at Summit Springs. Carr struck forcefully, and in a hard, day-long fight, fifty-two Cheyennes— including Tall Bull—were killed, and their entire village and belongings destroyed. The survivors staggered away and sought refuge among the Sioux on the White River.

The defeat of Tall Bull's band ended Cheyenne residence in the country between the Platte and the Arkansas. This land of western Kansas and eastern Colorado, once the stronghold of the Cheyenne Dog Soldiers, had now been wrested away by whites for their stage routes, railroads, forts, and settlements. The Dog Soldiers disbanded. Some went north and others remained south of the Arkansas River.

Meanwhile, the starving southern bands made their way to Camp Supply and placed themselves at the mercy of the U.S. government for food and shelter. There they would be under the guardianship of members of the *Quakers*, the Society of Friends, to whom President Ulysses S. Grant had been persuaded by peace proponents to assign the management of the nation's Indian tribes.

7

The Last Stand

The reservation area assigned to the Cheyennes and Arapahos by the Treaty of Medicine Lodge Creek in 1867 was situated in north-central Oklahoma. It was a poor location. The water there—supplied by the Salt Fork of the Arkansas River—was too brackish for the Indians and their horses, and the area was much too accessible to Osage horse thieves who lived nearby. The new Cheyenne agent, Brinton Darlington, a Quaker, eventually moved their agency south to the central Oklahoma area along the North Canadian River, near El Reno. This site soon became known as the Darlington Agency. President Grant then issued an executive order that gave the Cheyennes and Arapahos a new reservation area containing more than 4 million acres and extending west to the Texas panhandle.

Darlington was well into his sixties when he was appointed agent to the Southern Cheyennes and Arapahos, but he had the energy and hope of a younger man. He busily erected agency buildings: a school

Chief Stone Calf, pictured here with his wife, was one of the first Southern Cheyenne leaders to bring his people to the Darlington Reservation in Indian Territory (present-day Oklahoma). Despite agreeing to settle on the reservation, Stone Calf objected to the federal government's plan to make the Southern Cheyennes farmers.

for Indian children, in addition to offices, a dormitory, barns, stables, storehouses, and housing for himself and his staff. He also built a sawmill and broke ground to make way for corn fields and vegetable gardens. Like the other Quaker agents who arrived in Indian Territory, Darlington vowed to prove that the "Indian problem" could be handled peacefully.

Many impediments hampered his efforts. White traders still sneaked whiskey into Indian camps. Hunters descended on the great buffalo herds, destroying the tribe's prime game. Horse thieves—most of them white men—preyed upon Cheyenne herds. U.S. Army officers, resentful of the presence of the Quakers, opposed them at every turn. The toughest obstacle was posed by the Indians themselves, who balked at Quaker efforts to introduce their children to formal schooling and to turn proud hunters into farmers. Such leaders as Bull Bear and Medicine Arrows adamantly refused to bring their people into the new agency. Eventually, Stone Calf arrived with thirteen lodges, accompanied by John Simpson Smith and George Bent and their Cheyenne families.

Yet the majority of Southern Cheyennes remained afield, plagued both by hunger and diseases such as whooping cough and scarlet fever. Many children died during the winter of 1870–71. Cheyenne warriors joined in raiding parties against settlers in Texas and Kansas, and there was much talk of a new war.

Darlington died of natural causes in the spring of 1872. His fragile legacy of peace lasted through the year. The following winter, the Cheyennes managed to find and kill many buffalo and thus had enough to eat. But other problems persisted. Cheyenne women objected when their robes, the result of long, laborious effort, ended up in the hands of swindlers who duped Cheyenne men with whiskey. Pushed beyond the limit of their tolerance, the women refused to skin, tan, and sew any more hides into robes.

In Kansas, the Cheyennes learned that the first sign of trouble from whites was the arrival of U.S. government surveyors, who measured and mapped the land for railroads and settlement. The Cheyennes knew well that the surveyors' presence paved the way for white homesteaders who took away land that was rightfully theirs. They became fair game for Cheyenne warriors, and in the spring of 1873, a surveying party was massacred by Cheyennes near Camp Supply. Knowing that U.S. Army retaliation was inevitable, Cheyenne war factions led by Gray Beard, Bull Bear, Medicine Arrows, and others retreated to the upper Washita River.

The following autumn, agent John D. Miles tried to calm the situation by taking a group of chiefs to Washington, D.C. Even as they made their journey, a 160-man Cheyenne war party invaded Colorado, spoiling for a fight with the Utes living there. The frontier violence continued into 1874. Even the Darlington Agency was threatened, and some of its stock was run off by Cheyennes. After three settlers were slain near Medicine Lodge, Kansas, other homesteaders fled to safety.

In June 1874, a U.S. military detachment battled a party of Cheyennes and Kiowas above Camp Supply, and a party of white buffalo hunters was attacked near Adobe Walls in the Texas panhandle. Two of the hunters died. Later in the month, a combined force of Comanches, Kiowas, Arapahos, and Cheyennes surrounded the hunters' refuge in the ravine-slashed country of the Canadian River and made an unsuccessful attempt to overwhelm the makeshift fort. The Cheyennes lost six men in what became known as the Battle of Adobe Walls.

The next month, warriors struck a wagon train transporting goods north of the Darlington Agency. Three teamsters were shot and killed, and freighter Patrick Hennessey was tied to a wagon wheel and burned to death. In August, another surveying party was wiped out near Fort Dodge, Kansas.

The string of incidents proved a boon to General Sheridan, who could now argue effectively that Quaker appeasement policies had failed. The federal government gave him permission to plan a punitive campaign against the tribes. He devised a five-pronged attack. It included fighting units that set out from Fort Union in New Mexico, Fort Concho in Texas, Camp Supply, and Fort Sill. A final unit also drove westward between the latter two.

In August, Colonel Nelson A. Miles led a force on a south-western march into the Texas panhandle. There it subdued a large Cheyenne party and burned a few scattered villages before retiring from the area. A month later, another column of cavalry and infantry—led by Colonel Ranald S. Mackenzie—pushed south into the Texas panhandle and staged a surprise attack on a large village of combined tribes on the floor of Palo Duro Canyon. Most of the inhabitants escaped, but Mackenzie destroyed some four hundred lodges along with food supplies. He also captured 1,400 horses.

A still larger encampment was struck by forces under the command of Lieutanant Colonel George P. Buell, who destroyed five hundred tepees and seized many horses. The other prongs of Sheridan's campaign failed to engage the Cheyennes in major battles, though eventually the Fort Sill column, under Lieutenant Colonel J.W. Davidson, destroyed fifty Cheyenne lodges in the hills along the Red River.

Throughout 1874, Sheridan's army continued to harass the Cheyennes. The troops killed few Cheyennes, but they pushed families to the brink of starvation, destroyed their homes, and depleted their all-important horse herds and ammunition supplies. The Cheyennes could no longer hide, and by year's end many had surrendered.

In March 1875, the last 821 holdouts came into Darlington. Most turned in their arms, but several secretly held on to their rifles. Conflict arose when U.S. troops tried to place some Cheyenne chiefs and warriors in leg irons. A young warrior named Black Horse rebelled and tried to escape. Guards gunned him down. Other Cheyennes fired back and retreated to a sand hill near the agency. There they held off the troops until nightfall, when they fled north.

Some were intercepted and killed by U.S. troops on the Smoky Hill River in western Kansas. Most of the others were eventually rounded up again, and the military resumed its plan to punish the war leaders. Thirty-one men and a woman were selected, placed in irons, and shipped by railway car to prison at Fort Marion, Florida. One of them, Chief Gray Beard, was shot and killed en route when he jumped off the train and attempted to escape.

Thus concluded the last major show of resistance by the Southern Cheyennes. Their reign over the prairie had ended, their days of freedom gone forever. They were now at the mercy of the U.S. government.

The Northern Cheyennes, however, had not given up the fight. They loved the high country of the upper Missouri River. They felt spiritually linked to the beautiful mountains and valleys cut by bubbling icy-watered streams and teeming with bear, elk, caribou, and other wild game. It pained the Northern Cheyennes that these natural beauties and resources were threatened by white intruders. First came the multitude of immigrants who crossed their land on the way to Utah, California, and Oregon. Next came forts and soldiers. Then, in the 1860s, gold was discovered in western Montana, and prospectors flooded into territory where the Sioux, Northern Arapahos, and Northern Cheyennes hunted and camped. The Indians suffered again in 1866, when the U.S. government opened three new forts on the Bozeman Trail, which cut north from Colorado through Wyoming into Montana.

Northern Cheyenne warriors joined the Sioux leader Red Cloud, who attacked the forts as well as the transports that traveled between them. On December 21, 1866, the allied tribes laid siege to Fort Phil Kearny, located on the Powder River just east of the Big Horn Mountains in northern Wyoming. Two Northern Cheyenne chiefs, Little Wolf and Dull Knife (or Morning Star), served as war leaders.

For some time the Indians had been attacking small groups near the fort and making off with horses and cattle. When U.S. troops left the fort to search for them, the war parties always retreated. Their purpose was to lure troops into a trap, where a large warrior force could attack them. They repeated this pattern

Dull Knife (seated) and Little Wolf were among the Northern Cheyennes who settled with the Sioux on the Red Cloud Agency in Dakota Territory in the late 1860s. In 1873, the U.S. government threatened to remove them to the Southern Cheyennes' reservation in Indian Territory, and though the Northern Cheyennes resisted for a few years, they were eventually forced to join them in 1877.

until one morning when a sizable woodcutting detachment, traveling in several wagons, emerged from the fort. Little Wolf and Dull Knife sent a small war party to waylay it. The wagon train drew into a defensive circle until more troops from the fort arrived. The detachment then proceeded on toward the piney woods.

At the same time, another Indian party, mounted on swift horses, attacked the wagon train and then retreated into the nearby hills, hotly pursued by the troops. The soldiers followed—into an ambush. A much larger force of Indians set upon them and forced the troops to dismount and fight on foot. All eighty-one soldiers, led by Lieutenant W.J. Fetterman, were killed.

The Fetterman Massacre, as it became known, spurred the U.S. government to make new peace overtures to the northern Plains tribes. In 1868, the United States agreed to abandon the forts on the Bozeman Trail and withdraw its troops. Two new agencies, Spotted Tail and Red Cloud, were established for the Indians. Both were ultimately located on the White River of South Dakota. The Northern Cheyennes rejected any attempt to place them on a reservation and continued to roam about the Yellowstone and Bighorn country of northern Wyoming. Occasionally they visited Sioux and Gros Ventres at the agencies, but mostly they wandered, hunted, and raided the Crows and Shoshones as they had in years past.

By 1873, the membership rolls at the Red Cloud Agency, prepared by the Bureau of Indian Affairs, listed 1,900 Northern Cheyennes. The U.S. government planned to move them to Oklahoma, where the Southern Cheyennes were located. Northern Cheyenne leaders Little Wolf, Dull Knife, and others balked. They loved their homeland, they said, and preferred to die there rather than to leave it. In November 1873, a delegation of Northern Cheyennes went to Washington, D.C., to meet with President Grant. Grant told them that the treaty they had signed in 1868 forced them to accept the move south. He was wrong: The treaty did not commit the tribe to move; it only expressed the desire of the United States that they do so. The chiefs had never agreed to it. As a result, the Northern Cheyennes were able to resist deportation for the time being.

The following year, Lieutenant Colonel Custer led an exploratory expedition into the Black Hills, an area in the Dakotas long considered a sanctuary by the Cheyennes, Arapahos, and Sioux. Not only did Custer's incursion incense the tribes, it led to the discovery of gold and an ensuing rush there by white miners in 1875. A number of prospectors and others were killed by Indians.

The U.S. government tried to purchase the Black Hills, but the tribes spurned their offers, and in the spring of 1876 the U.S. War Department drew up plans to contain and punish the tribes residing along the Yellowstone River. A three-strike campaign was conceived: General George Crook moved northwest from newly built Fort Fetterman, in Wyoming; General John Gibbon headed southeast from Fort Shaw, in Montana; and General Alfred Terry proceeded west from Fort Abraham Lincoln, in South Dakota.

On May 29, Crook left Fort Fetterman with fifteen troops of cavalry and five companies of infantry. They marched along the Tongue River, where on June 9 a war party attacked them. The party was small and easily repulsed, but another, more severe engagement with Northern Cheyennes and Sioux occurred a few days later at the head of the Rosebud River in southeastern Montana. Neither side prevailed, but Crook had to turn back in order to regroup his troops.

The Cheyenne and Sioux warriors returned to camps on the Little Bighorn River and held war dances. Meanwhile, General Terry had begun his push westward from Fort Abraham Lincoln. He took his infantry force up the Yellowstone by steamboat and sent the Seventh Cavalry, under the command of Custer, to scout overland. Custer had very nearly lost his post because of political disagreements with President Grant.

The two forces rejoined at the mouth of the Rosebud River. Custer conferred with Terry aboard the steamboat *Far West* and was ordered to follow a broad Indian trail that wound along the Rosebud. At noon on June 22, Custer began his march with approximately six hundred troops, forty-four Indian scouts, and twenty or so packers (who carried supplies), guides, and civilians. Tom Custer, the lieutenant colonel's brother, commanded C Company, while another brother, Boston Custer, came along as packmaster—a civilian role.

On June 24, Custer reached a point where the Indian trail veered abruptly away from the Rosebud and snaked westward toward the Little Bighorn valley. Custer followed this trail, making camp that night on a ridge that divided the Rosebud and the Little Bighorn. The next morning, his scouts observed smoke in the valley ahead.

Though Custer surmised that a sizable Indian camp was situated there, he had no inkling of the strength of the Sioux and Cheyenne forces. He did not know they had pushed Crook back; nor was he aware that some twelve thousand to fifteen thousand Indians—including about five thousand well-armed warriors—lay in wait for him. The majority of these forces were Sioux, but at the upper end of the camp was a fighting force of Northern Cheyennes bolstered by Southern Cheyenne warriors who had fled their reservation in Indian Territory.

In the past, Custer had been unable to pin down Plains Indians—as he approached, they would vanish on their fast horses. He now saw an opportunity to defeat them in pitched battle and feared that any delay would enable them to escape from the valley. He violated his orders to await Terry and attacked. He divided his command into three battalions, placing three companies under Major Marcus Reno, three more under Captain Frederick Benteen, and leading the remainder of the troops himself, except for one company that stayed in the rear to protect the pack train.

Benteen's battalion was dispatched to the left of the trail to scout, and Custer and Reno continued toward the Little Bighorn. About two miles from the river, a portion of the Indian village came into view. Quickly, without scouting the enemy camps or surveying the lay of the land, Custer ordered

Reno to cross the river and charge the lower end of the camp. He then led his own troops along the east bank of the Little Bighorn, which was severely cut with gullies. His strategy was to support Reno's attack by assaulting the flank and rear of the Indian stronghold.

Custer, accompanied by his personal aide and his bugler, rode to the top of a hill and lifted his field glasses to his eyes. He gazed down on several hundred tepees—only a portion of the village. He turned in his saddle and waved his hat to Reno's forces, who were charging hard on the south end of the camp. Before riding back to his command, Custer spoke to his aide, who quickly scribbled a note. This man handed it to the bugler and ordered him to rush it to Benteen, who was still scouring the country behind them. The note read: "Benteen. Come on. Big village. Be quick. Bring packs. P.S. Bring packs." The bugler hurried to the rear, noting as he passed that Reno's men had charged the village and engaged the Indians across the river. Reno, it turned out, had met far more resistance than anticipated. Before him swarms of Indians rose out of the grass, firing rifles. When his cavalry charge faltered, Reno ordered his men to dismount and fight on foot. The number of Indians steadily increased, and Reno had his men remount and retreat to the shelter of the bluffs across the river.

Shortly after 3:00 P.M., Custer's bugler located Benteen, whose horses had struggled through the rough terrain. Benteen now pushed forward rapidly, joining Reno just as the latter's battalion, depleted and unnerved, reached the bluffs. The combined units were pinned down by Indian snipers. One company attempted to advance along the river bluffs and join Custer, but it was halted by a barrage of bullets from Indian rifles. As darkness loomed, Reno and Benteen ordered their men to retreat to a more tenable position in the bluffs. Their soldiers were unable to join Custer's portion of the Seventh Cavalry.

About the time that Reno had made his retreat, Custer and his 225 troops picked their way along the gully-cut ridge opposite the Indian camp and reached a point of descent leading to a place where the river could be crossed. As the troops neared the crossing, they were swarmed upon by Sioux, led by the warrior Gall. Two companies of troops dismounted for hand-to-hand combat, while Custer withdrew to a hilltop where he assumed a defensive position.

Some Indian sharpshooters zeroed in on horsemen. Others stampeded the cavalry packhorses that carried the vital ammunition supply for Custer's troops. At the same time Gall, now supported by warriors who had repulsed Reno, made a frontal attack from the south. The Northern Cheyennes under Brave Wolf and Lame White Man struck Custer's right flank and more Cheyennes attacked from the rear.

Custer was caught in a murderous crossfire as the warriors—superior in numbers and arms—made their charge. It probably did not take long—an hour or less—for the Sioux and Northern Cheyennes to overrun the embattled remnants of Custer's Seventh Cavalry. When General Terry finally arrived on June 27 to relieve Reno and Benteen, who were still pinned down, he found a terrible scene of carnage. The Indians, warriors and women alike, had swarmed over the battlefield, counting coup, stripping the dead troopers of their clothes and belongings, and shooting the near-dead and already dead. Custer, while stripped of his clothing, had not been scalped or mutilated, nor had most of his troops. The disaster of June 25, 1876, shocked the United States—not only the government but also ordinary citizens. To this day, "Custer's Last Stand" remains one of the most celebrated events of the Old West, the topic of fiction, films, and ongoing debate: Was Custer betrayed by his own vanity or by the incompetence of his subordinates?

The Little Bighorn was also the last glorious stand of Cheyenne warriors. After defeating Custer, the Northern Cheyennes withdrew deep into the wild country, aware that the whites would seek to avenge the grave loss. They were right. A

This drawing by Oglala Sioux artist Amos Bad Heart Buffalo depicts the retreat of U.S. Army Major Marcus Reno during the Battle of the Little Bighorn on June 25, 1876. A combined force of Arapaho, Northern Cheyenne, and Sioux warriors defeated the U.S. Army, which was under the command of Lieutenant Colonel George Armstrong Custer, who was killed during the battle.

new expedition was organized almost immediately under General Ranald S. Mackenzie. His first objective was to capture Red Cloud's village of Sioux, which was assigned to the Pine Ridge Agency. He accomplished this quickly in 1876 and then left Fort Fetterman and moved northward toward the Powder River in Wyoming. On November 26, Mackenzie's troops, supported by Pawnee scouts plus Shoshones and Bannocks, located and surrounded Dull Knife's village of Northern Cheyennes on the Crazy Woman Fork of the Powder. In a dawn attack, they assaulted and destroyed the village, overcoming fierce resistance.

The survivors fled into the snowbound hills and canyons. Many—including Dull Knife and Little Wolf—eventually found refuge with the Sioux. Despite that tribe's hospitality, the Cheyennes sank into destitution. They possessed few horses, robes, or blankets and had no food. They struggled through a terrible winter, and in April 1877, Dull Knife was forced to surrender at Fort Robinson, Nebraska. Other Cheyennes also turned themselves over to U.S. authorities.

Now the U.S. government could accomplish by force what it had failed to do by treaty—remove the Cheyennes of the north and consolidate them with the Southern Cheyennes in Indian Territory. When the Northern Cheyennes still refused to leave their beloved high country, their food rations were withheld. Finally they agreed to go, but only on a trial basis.

During the summer and early fall, about one thousand Northern Cheyennes began a grueling seventy-day trek from Fort Robinson, in the northern tip of Nebraska, to the Darlington Agency near El Reno, Oklahoma. They walked under a blazing sun, and nearly two-thirds of the group were stricken by an epidemic of fever and ague. The survivors vowed that someday they would make it back home.

8

Agency Life

As bad as reservation life in Indian Territory was for the Southern Cheyennes, it proved much worse for the Northern Cheyennes. They were sad to leave the high, dry country of the North, with its ample reserves of game, for the humid flatlands almost bereft of buffalo and deer. Hunger and sickness haunted them during the winter of 1877–78 and into the following summer. Despair sharpened Cheyenne resistance to the U.S. government's plans to turn them into farmers and to indoctrinate them into a new way of life.

As conditions worsened, the Northern Cheyenne chiefs plotted a return to their home ranges. "I am going north to my own country," Chief Little Wolf told Agent John D. Miles. "I do not want to see blood spilt about this agency. Let me get a little distance away from this agency. Then if you want to fight, I will fight you, and we can make the ground bloody at that place."

On the night of September 7, 1878, some 353 Northern

Cheyennes left their campfires burning and tepee poles standing and began the trek north under Little Wolf, Dull Knife, and other chiefs. They had gone only a short distance when the alarm sounded behind them. Two troops of the Fourth Cavalry, led by Captain Joseph Rendlebrock, hotly pursued them. Two days later the enemies fought at Turkey Springs, north of the Cimarron River. The Cheyenne warrior force—which included about 160 men and boys—held off the soldiers, killing three and wounding three more. Five Cheyennes were badly hurt.

The Cheyennes fled north into Kansas and again were intercepted, this time by Camp Supply troops who met them south of the Arkansas River. Little Wolf led a charge against the U.S. Army supply wagons and captured some ammunition. The Cheyennes wanted to avoid a major struggle, however, and withdrew from the field at dark. They pressed northward, traveling through the night. On the Arkansas River, the Cheyennes met and captured a group of buffalo hunters. Little Wolf ordered them released without harm and took only eighteen slaughtered buffalo for his people to eat.

While still in Kansas, the Cheyennes met a third detachment of troops. The Cheyennes prevailed again, routing the enemy with close-range gunfire. The exodus continued into northwestern Kansas, where the Cheyennes came upon civilians along the Sappa and Beaver rivers. The Indians slew some white men for their horses but did not harm women or children.

Finally, the Northern Cheyennes entered the country beyond the Platte River, in Nebraska, and there divided into two groups. Little Wolf took one contingent to the Powder River country—in Wyoming and Montana—where they surrendered peacefully to U.S. troops. Later, Little Wolf and some of his men served as scouts for General Nelson A. Miles in his war against the Sioux. The second group of Cheyennes—about 150 strong—followed Dull Knife to the Red Cloud Agency near Fort Robinson, Nebraska. They surrendered, yielded their arms, and were held prisoner in a large, unheated building.

Soon conditions became unbearable. The Cheyennes went seven days without fire, food, or water, and many froze and starved. In desperation, they decided to face the soldiers' bullets or to brave the weather outdoors rather than perish helplessly inside the building. On January 9, 1879, Dull Knife's people made a frantic charge for freedom. They leaped from the windows of their prison and dashed toward the surrounding hills. A few of the warriors had secretly hidden guns in the folds of the women's clothing. They now used them to fend off the soldiers while their women and children escaped.

The heroic attempt failed. Sixty-five of the 150 Cheyennes were recaptured, many of them wounded, and the frozen bodies of 50 more were found in the nearby hills by a detail of soldiers. Some Cheyennes disappeared altogether. The survivors were sent to the Pine Ridge Agency and assigned to their own agency in Montana. A few of the chiefs involved in the Northern Cheyenne's flight were later taken to Fort Dodge, Kansas, to be tried for the murder of a white man. The charges were eventually dropped, and the chiefs returned to Indian Territory and accepted the fate of reservation life.

While Dull Knife and his people were being held at Fort Robinson, the U.S. government shifted another large group of Northern Cheyennes, led by Little Chief, south to Indian Territory. Little Chief's band encountered the same oppressive conditions faced by their northern kin: sickness, scant food, cornmeal that made them sick, resentment by the Southern Cheyennes, and pressure from agents to adopt a way of life they detested.

Little Chief spoke for his people when he told the agent: "I was in good condition then [in the North]; now, look and see how poor I am growing since I came down here. . . . We all would rather be among those mountains and streams where we were raised. . . . we never get sick there. I was used to living by

Little Chief and his band of Northern Cheyennes were moved to the Southern Cheyenne reservation in 1877, but after traveling to Washington, D.C., in 1879, Little Chief was able to persuade the U.S. government to allow his band to settle on the Pine Ridge Reservation in Dakota Territory in 1881.

hunting all the time. It does not make me feel good to hang about an agency and have to beg a white man for something to eat when I get hungry."

Little Chief struggled to restrain his warriors during the next two years of hardship and difficulty, and in 1879 the

Cheyenne leader took his case to Washington, D.C. He persuaded U.S. authorities to allow him and his people back on the Pine Ridge Agency, though they did not receive formal permission to return there until 1881.

During the 1880s, the Cheyennes still living in Indian Territory fell victim to broken promises and self-contradictory government policies. Unable to hunt buffalo, which had been wiped off the Western plains by hordes of white hunters, the Indians grew increasingly dependent on the U.S. government. At the same time, they suffered continued mistreatment by whiskey dealers, unscrupulous traders, and white horse thieves.

Agent Miles initiated several programs meant to aid the Cheyennes. Some met with more success than others. Efforts to make farmers of Cheyenne men did not work, and after several years the idea was abandoned. Miles had better luck with the Cheyenne-Arapaho Transportation Company. This project called for the hiring of Cheyennes and Arapahos as teamsters, or wagon drivers, who hauled their own goods and other freight from Kansas railheads to the agency. Miles purchased forty wagons and harnesses, and soon Indian teamsters regularly drove the trail in Kansas between the Darlington Agency, Wichita, and Arkansas City.

Miles had another promising idea—establishing a cattle herd on the agency. He reasoned that it would feed the tribe and also train Cheyenne youths in stock tending and ranching. He was proved right on both counts as the herd grew in size and helped avert a food crisis. Then officials in Washington, D.C., leveled charges of corruption against the agency and ordered an end to Indian cattle raising. Miles then set up a policy whereby the Cheyennes leased grasslands to outside cattlemen. Again he was foiled: Officials ordered him to rid the reservation of all cattle not owned by the Indians. Eventually Miles overcame this opposition, and the Cheyennes developed a sizable operation. However, troubles arose between the Indians and the cattlemen, and criticism of the program persisted until Miles was forced to resign in 1884.

His replacement, D.B. Dyer, reverted to the old policy of making farmers out of the Cheyennes. They resisted strongly, led by Stone Calf and Little Robe. The Dog Soldiers, only some of whom had disbanded, remained a serious hindrance to Dyer's efforts. They destroyed fences, killed cattle and horses, and threatened fellow Cheyennes with serious harm. Tensions mounted, and additional troops were brought into Fort Reno, which sat just across the North Canadian River from Darlington.

In July 1885, generals Philip Sheridan and Nelson Miles arrived to investigate the problem. Sheridan let the Cheyennes and cattlemen voice their complaints, but this attempt at fair-mindedness was undercut by President Grover Cleveland, who summarily ordered the reservation cleared of non-Indian cattle. A new agent, Captain Jesse M. Lee, replaced Dyer and removed some 210,000 head of cattle from Indian land. Cheyenne chiefs and the Dog Soldiers took solace in having thwarted the U.S. government.

This victory was short-lived. The entire structure of Cheyenne society would soon be imperiled. The first blow came in 1887 with the passage of the Dawes, or General Allotment, Act. This federal legislation decreed that the president could allot reservation lands owned collectively by the tribe to individual tribe members, whom it reclassified as landowners and then as citizens subject to the laws of the state or territory where they lived. The act also provided for the sale of surplus reservation lands to whites.

The Dawes Act scattered the Southern Cheyennes on clusters of small farms along the North Canadian, South Canadian, and Washita rivers. This fragmented the tribe, unhinged its social structure, and blunted the influence of chiefs and war societies. Internal strife and factionalism now weakened the tribe. The Cheyennes forsook their own ceremonies and

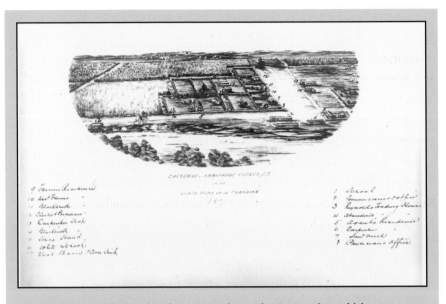

This 1878 drawing depicts the Cheyenne and Arapaho Reservation, which was located on the North Fork of the Canadian River in what is today Oklahoma. In 1887, the Dawes Act allotted 160 acres to adult males who lived on the reservation, thus opening up the surplus reservation land to white settlers. As a result, many Southern Cheyennes were scattered about, mostly along the North Canadian, South Canadian, and Washita rivers.

became caught up in the *Ghost Dance religion*, which was made popular in the late 1880s by the Paiute medicine man Wovoka. He and his priests claimed to have conversed with Christ, who granted them a vision that predicted the removal of whites from Indian Country within two years and a return to the old days of the buffalo hunts and Indian supremacy. When the two years were up, however, neither prediction had come true, and the Ghost Dance fell out of favor among most tribes.

In 1889, on the heels of the Dawes Act, came another crushing blow: the opening up to white settlement of the Unassigned Lands, which lay in the heart of Indian Territory and abutted the Cheyenne-Arapaho Reservation (known by this time as the "Oklahoma Country"). A tumultuous land rush ensued. Then the U.S. government tried to purchase the surplus Cheyenne-Arapaho reservation lands from the tribes. Chief Old Crow spoke for his people when he told U.S. commissioners: "The Great Spirit gave the Indians all this country and never tell them that they should sell it. . . . I don't want money; money doesn't do an Indian any good."

U.S. government pressure proved too much, and a sale agreement was eventually reached, though the Cheyennes challenged its validity, arguing that the document had not been signed by 75 percent of adult males, as required by law. Nonetheless, Congress approved the Cheyenne-Arapaho cession pact on March 3, 1891, and the era of the reservation came to an end for the southern tribes.

A year later, when the Cheyenne-Arapaho Reservation was opened to white settlement, the amount of land still controlled by the tribes had been reduced from more than 4 million acres to 529,692 acres. Much of what remained would be lost in the years ahead through a variety of tactics, including illegal taxation, crooked business dealings, and outright thievery. The Indians tried to protect themselves, but they stood no chance of gaining justice in the biased courts of the recently established Oklahoma Territory.

As if these setbacks were not enough, the entire culture of the Cheyennes came under attack in the 1890s when agent A.E. Woodson, a stern former military officer, campaigned to diminish the power of Cheyenne chiefs. He stripped their authority to issue rations within their tribe and thus humbled chiefs into standing in line with their followers for handouts. He outlawed sacred Cheyenne ceremonies, such as the Sun Dance and Medicine Arrow rites. He dispersed the Indians onto individual and isolated land allotments in order to break up their communal camp life. He also sought to stop gambling and the use of *peyote*, the drug introduced to Cheyenne culture that was part of many religious ceremonies, including the Ghost Dance. Finally, Woodson invoked territorial law to prohibit Cheyenne men from keeping more than one wife at a time.

Old Crow and other chiefs strenuously resisted this attack on their way of life, and most Southern Cheyennes clung to their accustomed ways. The odds were stacked against them. It was easier to become a farmer or to seek out the few jobs offered by white society than to practice older customs. Some Cheyennes began to abandon their habitual style of dress, cut their long hair, move into wood-frame houses instead of tepees, and bow to the restraints and laws of the larger society that surrounded them.

Similar difficulties and upheavals beset the Northern Cheyennes. In 1884, they had been given a small reservation on the Tongue River in Montana, and in the years that followed they subsisted on wild berries and fruits and killed the few animals that still roamed free. By century's end, the Northern Cheyennes turned to farming, raising corn and other vegetables as they had done more than one hundred years earlier before they became buffalo hunters.

As well as they could, they lived off the land. They cut hay from the rich grasslands of their reservation and sold it to nearby ranchers. They sold firewood and worked as wagon drivers. They also continued to thrive as horse breeders. They expertly tended the few beasts they had taken with them to the reservation and produced fine herds that brought good prices from ranchers and the U.S. cavalry.

In the early 1900s, the U.S. government furnished individual Northern Cheyennes with small starting herds of cows and bulls, and their situation improved greatly. The men soon proved themselves as capable with cattle as with horses, and the size of their herds steadily increased. This new prosperity was halted in 1914, when the Bureau of Indian Affairs decreed that the individually owned herds had to be consolidated into a single tribal herd. This mandate embittered Cheyenne cattle owners, who had to choose between relinquishing their herds or watching them be removed by soldiers. Thieves, hard winters, and wolves soon depleted the herd. It was hit particularly hard and greatly reduced during the bitterly cold winters of 1919 and 1920.

The situation grew worse in 1919 when the BIA decreed that a large number of Cheyenne horses would have to be destroyed in order to make more grassland available to the cattle herds. Many of the horses were shot, and their meat became rations for the tribe. Others were sold off—without a cent of the proceeds going to the Cheyennes. Their herd shrank from fifteen thousand head to three thousand, an incalculable loss to the horse-loving tribe.

Shortly after their horses disappeared, so too did their land. In the 1920s, the U.S. government tried to persuade the Northern Cheyennes to divide their reservation by allotting portions of land to individuals. Initially the Cheyennes staunchly opposed the arrangement, but eventually accepted it in 1933. Each member received 160 acres, and less than half the total land remained under tribal control.

In the late nineteenth and early twentieth century, the Northern Cheyennes struggled to keep alive their ancestral culture. The forces ranged against them were powerful. The most insistent call of white authorities was that Cheyennes be sent to school, a concession the Dog Soldiers fought by pressuring their people to maintain their traditional ways. By the 1880s, peace chiefs began to soften their opposition, and a few children appeared in classrooms. A mission school opened at Darlington in 1881, run by the Mennonite Church, and another school opened at the former U.S. Army post at Cantonment, northwest of Darlington. Eventually, some Cheyenne boys went to Carlisle Indian School in Pennsylvania and Hampton Institute in Virginia.

Only a small minority of Cheyenne children received schooling, however. In 1889, it was estimated that only one out of six Cheyennes knew the English language well enough to speak or understand it, and only about a quarter of those had much formal schooling. As for the rest, once they graduated, they remained outsiders, shut out of the American mainstream. Most went back home and resumed their lives within the tribe.

In subsequent decades, the Southern and Northern Cheyennes suffered setbacks, but they came to contrasting fates. Throughout most of the twentieth century, the Southern Cheyennes lived in poverty and suffered the prejudice of their white neighbors. However, more opportunities became available to them than in previous times and a greater percentage of Southern Cheyennes now receive an education and pursue the material rewards long scorned by the tribe. As jobs became available outside their tribal lands in south-central Oklahoma, their population dropped—from 6,674 in 1970 to 5,220 in 1985.

The Northern Cheyennes have enjoyed much greater prosperity. In the late 1960s, vast quantities of coal were discovered beneath the soil of their reservation in the southeastern part of Montana. There was a great demand for this mineral, and the Northern Cheyennes saw history repeat itself as their land was overrun by new invaders, this time huge coal and energy corporations working in league with a longtime foe, the U.S. government. Yet again, the Cheyennes were taken advantage of by those supposed to aid them: On the advice of the BIA, they signed away the mineral rights to more than half their reservation in return for large bonuses offered by the coal companies.

Soon they realized that the companies' plans for massive strip mines and power plants could mean the destruction of their land. They enlisted the help of George Crossland, a young BIA staff lawyer and an Osage. He advised them of illegal provisions in the contracts they had signed, and the Northern Cheyennes petitioned for the agreements to be cancelled. They did not regain everything they sought, but managed to protect their land and environment and to ensure themselves a secure future. At last, they scored a clear victory against their oppressors and exercised control over their own lives. For this reason, the population of the Northern Cheyenne Reservation climbed from 2,100 in 1970 to 3,177 in 1985.

During the last couple of decades of the twentieth century, both branches of the Cheyenne nations inhabited a world defined partly by white society and partly by their own traditions. They drive automobiles, eat hamburgers, and enjoy popular music. They also hold traditional powwows and cherish their ancestral celebrations, dances, songs, and games. Some Cheyennes rue the dimming of cherished tribal lore and blame the influence of white society. Others blame the tribe itself for giving in to the demands of the larger culture. In any case, the choice between the present and the past is not an easy one for a people who have become aliens in a land they once claimed as their own.

9

The Tsetschestahase in the Twenty-First Century

The modern Cheyenne nations took shape at the end of the nineteenth century, the result of federal Indian policies that sought to remake Cheyenne life in the mold of white Americans'. Though separated by geography, the Northern and the Southern Cheyenne people, known as the *Tsetschestahase* in the Cheyenne language, maintained cultural and spiritual ties by holding ceremonies and remaining in contact, and considered themselves related through language, tradition, and history. They maintain those ties today, to varying degrees.

The Northern Cheyenne Reservation in Montana was created by a federal government executive order in November 1884, and then expanded by another executive order of March 1900. It is a small reservation of only 440,000 acres. Unlike many other Indian reservations, nearly all of the reservation land is owned by Cheyennes; in contrast, many whites own significant portions of other reservations'

94

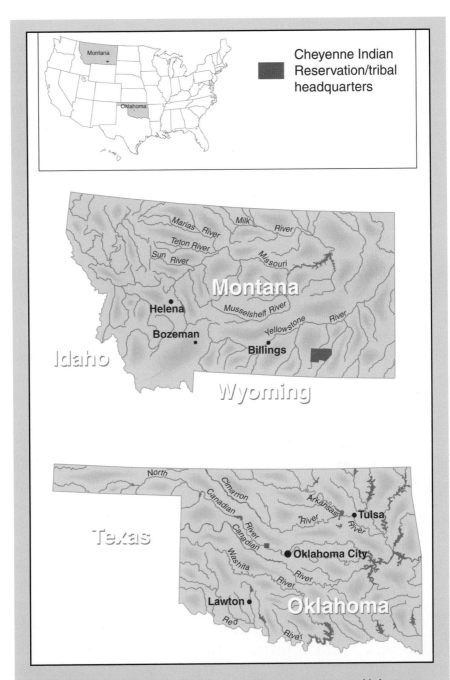

The Northern Cheyenne Reservation lies in southeastern Montana and is home to approximately 4,500 Cheyennes. The Southern Cheyennes no longer have a reservation, but their headquarters, which they share with the Southern Arapahos, is in Concho, Oklahoma.

land base by way of purchasing Indians' allotments. Since 1960, when tribal President John Woodenlegs initiated his land consolidation program, the Northern Cheyenne tribe has worked to purchase non-Indian landholdings.

As of 2000, 4,470 Cheyennes live on the reservation, with another 2,030 Cheyennes living off the reservation. Every four years eligible voters elect fellow Cheyennes to the Northern Cheyenne Tribal Council, which operates under a constitution established in 1935 as part of the Indian Reorganization Act. The tribe elected its first woman president in 2000. The council is made up of ten members, in addition to the president and the vice-president. It meets twice a month to resolve tribal members' disputes, set economic and social policy, and negotiate with outside vendors, including the federal government.

In Oklahoma, the Southern Cheyennes share tribal administration with the Southern Arapahos (whose northern counterparts live on the Wind River Reservation in Wyoming); the total enrollment of both tribes in 2004 was 11,627. The two tribes originally owned a 5-million-acre reservation, but the federal government broke it up through *Allotment.* An Act of March 3, 1891, divided Cheyenne-Arapaho land into 160-acre parcels. The remainder was sold to white homesteaders. As a result of these policies, the Southern Cheyennes do not have a reservation as such. The Cheyenne-Arapahos are recognized as an official Indian tribe and thus maintain all the rights accorded to Native Americans, despite the lack of a reservation. At the tribal headquarters in Concho, Oklahoma, the Cheyenne-Arapaho Business Committee runs tribal affairs; the business committee consists of eight members from four districts and includes four Cheyenne and four Arapaho representatives. This committee operates under the provisions of the Cheyenne-Arapaho Constitution and By-Laws, which tribal voters ratified on April 19, 1975.

In 1997, several descendants of the Southern Cheyennes sought to split the Cheyenne-Arapaho tribes and create a sovereign Cheyenne Nation distinct from the Cheyenne-Arapahos. Marcianna Little Man Jacobs organized the initiative, arguing that she and others "resent" being called Cheyenne-Arapahos. "We are Cheyenne," she said. The Cheyenne-Arapaho tribe debated separating the Cheyennes and Arapahos in the early 1970s and then again in 1994, but no changes were made. Cheyenne-Arapaho leaders claim that few tribal members support this initiative. "There are just a handful of people in our tribe who are trying to do this," said Archie Hoffman, the Cheyenne-Arapaho business secretary. Others oppose the split because of the number of tribal members who consider themselves both Arapahos and Cheyennes. "I'm against it because I have children who are Cheyenne and Arapaho," said Cheyenne-Arapaho Election Board Chairwoman June Black Black, a full-blood Arapaho.

Cheyennes also live in other Western states, especially Colorado, where roughly 3,000 Cheyennes lived in the mid-1800s. As of 2002, 328 full-blooded Cheyennes lived in Colorado, which has important significance for even those Cheyennes who live in Oklahoma or Montana because of the trauma of being violently wrenched from their homeland there after the 1864 Sand Creek Massacre. Calling Colorado "our beloved homeland," University of Montana Native American studies professor Henrietta Mann, a Northern Cheyenne, argued that "Colorado still figures very prominently in my sense of identity as a Cheyenne person"; in 1991, *Rolling Stone* magazine placed Mann in the top ten of professors in the United States. Some of Mann's ancestors survived the brutal attack of white militia on Cheyenne men, women, and children at Sand Creek. Montoya Whiteman also has ancestors who survived that massacre. Part Cheyenne and part Arapaho, Whiteman was born in Oklahoma, moved to Montana, and then found herself drawn to Denver, where she has worked as a spokeswoman for the Native American Rights Fund. Ms. Whiteman still travels back to Montana for

Cheyenne ceremonies, but in moving to Denver she "came back to my roots. . . . I don't want my traditions to die. I want to help my culture survive."

A famous Cheyenne proverb holds that, "A nation is not conquered until the hearts of its women are on the ground. Then it is finished, no matter how brave its warriors, or how strong their weapons." Henrietta Mann and Montoya Whiteman are just a few of the many Cheyenne women who are leading efforts to help their culture survive. They include Carol Redcherries, who in 1996 gave a talk at the Autry Museum of Western Heritage in Los Angeles, explaining to the audience that Native American women play an important role in preserving Indian traditions. Redcherries had served in the U.S. Army, in the Middle East, and then returned to the reservation with a law degree to become the chief justice of the Northern Cheyenne Appellate Court and a tribal elder. Another prominent Cheyenne woman is Susan Harjo. Harjo, of Cheyenne and Hodulgee Muscogee descent, helped author the 1990 *Native American Graves Protection and Repatriation Act*; 1989 National Museum of the American Indian Act; and the 1978 American Indian Religious Freedom Act. Ms. Harjo is a columnist for *Indian Country Today*, the leading Native American newspaper, and the president of the Morning Star Institute, which focuses on fighting stereotypical and discriminatory images in American popular culture and media.

Other prominent Cheyennes have supported these efforts to preserve and protect their traditions. Ben Nighthorse Campbell, the former U.S. Senator from Colorado, is an enrolled member of the Northern Cheyenne Nation. Campbell served in Korea during the Korean War, captained the U.S. judo team at the 1964 Olympic Games, then became a self-employed jewelry designer, rancher, and horse trainer before beginning his political career. Retired from the U.S. Senate, Campbell serves on the forty-four-member Council of Chiefs of the Southern Cheyenne and Northern Cheyenne people. Senator

Former Colorado Senator Ben Nighthorse Campbell (left) is shown here dressed in traditional Cheyenne clothing during the groundbreaking of the National Museum of the American Indian in Washington, D.C., in September 1999. Seated next to Campbell is Hawaii Senator Daniel Inouye, who chaired the Committee on Indian Affairs from 1987 to 1995.

Campbell supported the efforts of W. Richard West and of Susan Harjo to create the new National Museum of the American Indian, which opened on the National Mall in Washington, D.C., in September 2004. W. Richard West, who was educated at Harvard and Stanford, serves as the first museum director, as well as a Southern Cheyenne peace chief.

Harjo and West also have been leaders in Native Americans' efforts to preserve Native culture and identity through the repatriation (or return) of objects and ancestral remains held by the U.S. government or private collectors. For West, the son of a prominent Cheyenne artist and a music teacher of Scottish descent, "Repatriation is the most potent political metaphor for cultural revival that is going on at this time. Political sovereignty and cultural sovereignty are linked inextricably, because the ultimate goal of political sovereignty is the protecting of a way of life." The Repatriation movement addressed the historical legacy of the 1800s. As white settlers, soldiers, and scientists fanned out over the United States in the nineteenth century they came across or actively searched for Indian burial sites, which contained an array of cultural items, such as pots, arrowheads and clothes, skeletal remains, and the sacred objects used in Indian ceremonies, including those used in the funeral ceremony itself, called funerary objects. "Body snatching," as many Native Americans call it, became regularized in the mid-1800s. In one terrible case of the 1860s, at Sand Creek, more than 150 Cheyennes and Arapahos were slaughtered by the Colorado state militia, which sent a number of the bodies to the Smithsonian Institution for study, on orders of the U.S. Army.

In the late 1960s, according to a leader of the Repatriation movement, a Cheyenne elder maintained that "our nations couldn't heal and couldn't regain our strength and we as individuals couldn't heal until we recovered our dead relatives from these places and our sacred objects, our living beings." Demanding repatriation, tribal leaders went to Congress in the 1980s to appeal for federal help. In 1987, Northern Cheyenne spiritual leader Bill Tall Bull asked a Senate committee, "How would you feel if your grandmother's grave were opened, the contents were shipped back east to be boxed and warehoused with 31,000 others. . . . and itinerant pot-hunters were allowed to ransack her house in search of 'artifacts' with the blessing of the U.S. government? It is uncivilized . . . savage . . . inhuman . . . It is un-Christian." From this testimony and with help from Cheyennes like Harjo and West, Congress passed into law the landmark Native American Graves Protection and Repatriation Act (NAGPRA). NAGPRA created new codes for protecting Indian gravesites by raising civil and criminal penalties for the "illegal trafficking" of Native American remains and artifacts. NAGPRA also required a federal museum receiving federal funding to inventory its "human remains," "funerary objects," "sacred objects" ("ceremonial objects which are needed by traditional Native American religious leaders for the practice of traditional Native American religious"), and items of "cultural patrimony," defined as objects "having ongoing historical, traditional, or cultural importance, central to the Native American group or culture itself." In July 1992, the Cheyennes won the right to repatriate the remains of Cheyenne victims of the Sand Creek Massacre from the Smithsonian Institution.

Today, the Cheyennes continue to wrestle with difficult historical events such as the Sand Creek Massacre and the efforts of their nineteenth-century Cheyenne ancestors to preserve their independence. For example, roughly fifty runners participate in an annual Breakout Memorial Run, which covers four hundred miles from Fort Lincoln, Nebraska, to Busby, Montana, to memorialize the Cheyennes who died in 1879 trying to escape from captivity in Nebraska to reach their Montana homeland. One year, the youngest runner was eight years old, the oldest a grandfather. The runners covered the entire four hundred miles, even when the temperature dropped to twenty below zero and even when they ran into a blizzard in the Black Hills of South Dakota. According to Philip Whiteman, Jr., who organized the run, the participants are "sacrificing their bodies and their minds for the memory of their ancestors and to help themselves and their nation." Part of the healing comes from the fact that the runners finish their difficult four-hundred-mile journey at the ancestral burial ground where the bodies of the dead Cheyennes now rest; they had been resting in drawers and closets at the Smithsonian Institution until they were repatriated back to the Cheyennes in 1993. Many of the runners are direct descendants of those who were killed by U.S. soldiers. As a result, tribal spiritual advisor

Lee Lone Bear said, "Old people who take part in the ceremony cry with emotions that come from deep in their hearts. The older they are, the deeper their feelings. Some young ones cry, too." The run is designed in part to educate Northern Cheyenne youth, according to Lynette Two Bulls. "They need to learn about their history and where they come from—because that's who they are and they can't forget it. . . .—it puts self-esteem and pride back into our youth. They need to reconnect with who they are and their identity."

Cheyenne leaders emphasize educating young Cheyennes about the past to preserve identity, as well as educating them for the future. In an in-depth article in the 2003 issue of *Tribal College Journal of American Indian Higher Education*, Northern Cheyenne educator Richard Littlebear argued that "education can be our Buffalo," maintaining that it is "the key to the success" for Northern Cheyennes and for other Native Americans. "The students of today are going to be our leaders. . . . Our leaders have to know about the stock exchange, about cybernetic technology, about international markets and foreign affairs, about negotiating with large corporate entities, and about effectively developing and marketing our natural resources and our individual natural talents." The president of the Northern Cheyenne's Dull Knife Community College, Littlebear noted that tribal colleges and universities (*tcus*) provide an important basis for social, economic, and even spiritual progress because they offer "venues for strengthening our languages and cultures . . . by offering classes in indigenous languages, linguistics, and classroom methodologies." Littlebear should know. He obtained a bachelor's degree in English at Bethel College in Kansas, a master's degree in education at Montana State University, and then a doctorate in education from Boston University. Education will enable Northern Cheyennes to remain on the reservation, which offers access to "sacred places" and "deep spiritual connections."

Continued access to the sacred Cheyenne language also is

important for maintaining spiritual connections. According to Littlebear, the Cheyenne people need to balance the practical benefits that learning English provides with the spiritual benefits that relearning Cheyenne offers. He notes that the Cheyennes "must also promote English because it gives us physical sustenance and enables us to work in the present society; whereas Cheyenne provides us with spiritual sustenance, positively reinforces our identity, and lets us commune with all that we hold sacred. Both languages are useful in their unique ways and are equally important to us."

Roughly 40 percent of Northern Cheyennes speak the Cheyenne language; Southern Cheyennes also speak the language. Chief Dull Knife College has provided necessary space for preserving the language. With a grant from the W.K. Kellogg Foundation, officials of the college established a language education curriculum for young adults, few of whom know the language. Students have to learn to speak fluently and translate passages from English to Cheyenne without using English. Modern words are substituted for words that don't exist in the old Cheyenne language. Diabetes, for example, translates as "the sugar sickness" in Cheyenne. The Cheyenne language is marked by long words like *náohkêsáa'oné'seómepêhévetsêhésto'anéhe*, which translates in English as: "I truly do not pronounce Cheyenne well." Since 1996, the State of Montana has supported these efforts by approving teacher certification classification for Indian languages. Non-Cheyennes can also learn the language in Lame Deer by enrolling in immersion instruction summer camps.

Chief Dull Knife College, named for the great Cheyenne chief of the 1800s, was one of the first tribal colleges to open in the 1970s, offering its first courses in 1978. It originally trained Cheyenne young adults for work in various mining operations but soon developed a broader curriculum that offered associate degrees in Applied Science and Arts, as well as various vocational certificates in several skill areas. The

The Cheyenne Language

The Cheyenne language is now being taught in Cheyenne schools and summer language immersion programs. It is a complex language that several thousand Cheyennes speak in Montana, Oklahoma, and Colorado communities. This word set offers an introduction to the language. Other examples are available at Native Languages of the Americas: *http://www.native-languages.org/cheyenne_words.htm*

Cheyenne Word Set

English (Français)	Cheyenne
One (Un)	Na'ëstse
Two (Deux)	Néše
Three (Trois)	Na'he
Four (Quatre)	Neve
Five (Cinq)	Nóho
Man (Homme)	Hetane
Woman (Femme)	Hé'e
Dog (Chien)	Hotame or Oeškeso
Sun (Soleil)	É še'he
Moon (Lune)	Taa'é-eše'he
Water (Eau)	Mahpe
White (Blanc)	Vo'kome
Yellow (Jaune)	Heove
Red (Rouge)	Ma'ė
Black (Noir)	Mo'ohta
Eat (Manger)	Emese
See (Voir)	Evoohta
Hear (Écouter)	Enesta
Sing (Chanter)	Enemene
Leave (Partir)	Enoohta

college's mission statement says that the college intends to provide opportunities for Cheyennes to "equip themselves for a fulfilling life and responsible citizenship in a world characterized by change, while simultaneously studying and enhancing Cheyenne cultural values."

Getting Northern Cheyenne students to the college level has been a challenge, as school officials have had to contend with a high dropout rate. The Northern Cheyennes face the types of problems that non-Indian communities deal with, such as drug and alcohol problems. Tribal officials have made much progress. Between 2002 and 2004, the high school dropout rate fell from 17 percent to 6 percent. A federal grant helped to fund an alternative learning center that offers more flexible attendance, scheduling, and grading policies. Since 1993, a Boys and Girls Club has provided some recreational opportunities for Northern Cheyennes. The club has grown to two branches serving more than eight hundred Northern Cheyenne members between the ages of five and nineteen. The mission of the club, one of the first to form in Native American communities, is to promote "healthy lifestyles, social, educational, vocational, cultural, character and leadership development" and thus offer "a compelling alternative to crime, drugs, and other negative influences that impact our Reservation." To accomplish these goals, leaders of the club have staged an annual youth powwow every November, as well as other events that reinforce the values of the Cheyenne nation.

These powwows join other Northern Cheyenne festivals and celebrations, including the Memorial Day parade and rodeo, the Labor Day powwow, and the biggest event of all, the Fourth of July powwow, which includes dances, the Princess contest, food, and other activities. All of these events take place within an American context but are carried out with distinct Cheyenne traditions at their heart. In Oklahoma, the Southern Cheyennes also stage annual powwows and other cultural

For many Native Americans, including the Cheyennes, powwows are an important cultural expression. One of the most meaningful elements of powwows is dancing, which embodies indigenous values and is a way to express the tribe's survival.

events, including the Labor Day weekend powwow, the Cheyenne Homecoming Powwow, the American Indian Exposition, and the Sun Dance. Southern Cheyenne leader W. Richard West, Jr., noted that "dance is the very embodiment of indigenous values and represents the response of Native Americans to complex and sometimes difficult historical experiences. . . . The dance of native peoples is thus both a vital means of surviving culturally and a powerful expression of that survival."

Many of these dances are about Native Americans' special relationship with the land, captured in the long Cheyenne word *Xammaa-vo'estaneo'o*, which describes Cheyenne spiritual roots in the earth. Since the 1950s, the Northern Cheyennes have wrestled with the dilemma of how to preserve their land while also using it to create economic opportunities. Their negative experience with the federal government and with private energy companies in the 1960s and 1970s created a fear of large-scale energy development that remains today.

In the early 1970s, poor lease rates and environmental damage from mining prompted Native Americans around the country to reevaluate their policies of natural resource development. The Navajos faced environmental devastation from coal mining in the Black Mesa region of their reservation. The

Land Equals Life

John Woodenlegs emerged as the leader of the Northern Cheyenne tribe in the late 1950s during the Termination period in Native American history, when the federal government tried to end Indian sovereignty and dismantle their reservations. In this passage from a famous speech in 1960, he compares his struggle to prevent forced land sales with his ancestors' efforts to preserve the Cheyenne homeland. Woodenlegs advocated holding on to Cheyenne land and using it to benefit his people, emphasizing that the Cheyennes need land to remain Cheyenne.

I am not proud of myself for anything. I am a humble man. But I am proud to be a Cheyenne. In the old days my people fought hard to defend their homeland. The Cheyennes were a small tribe—but fast on horseback. They came and went like a tornado. That is why the soldiers shot down old people and children when defeat came. The soldiers did not stop until my people were helpless.... To us, being Cheyenne means one tribe—living on the land—in America, where we are citizens. Our land is everything to us. It is the only place in the world where Cheyennes talk the Cheyenne language to each other. It is the only place where Cheyennes remember the same things together. I will tell you one of the things we remember on our land. We remember our grandfathers paid for it—with their life.... Now you can understand why we are fighting to save our land today. This fight is not against soldiers. It is a fight to stop land sales.

Northern Cheyennes learned from the Navajo experience because they too owned huge coalfields and had also received below-market rates for coal in the 1960s. In 1972, a large energy company called Consolidation Coal (Consol) offered the Northern Cheyenne people big bonuses and royalties for the right to mine their coal and build four gasification plants on the reservation. Consol also offered to build a $1.5 million community health center. However, many Cheyennes thought that Consol's plan would ruin their reservation, as Consol would use valuable water resources for the gasification plants and would have to build a new town to house nearly thirty thousand workers, ten times the number of Cheyennes who lived on the reservation. The promise of nearly $500,000 per Cheyenne family failed to appeal to tribal members and they rejected Consol's offer, despite the poverty that gripped the reservation. One Cheyenne spoke for many of his fellow citizens when he noted that he would rather be poor on his land with his own people and thus protect the Cheyenne way of life rather than live rich on environmentally degraded land surrounded by strangers who did not respect that Cheyenne way of life.

Consol's offer made Northern Cheyenne officials understand exactly how valuable their coal was, and they moved to cancel all existing leases on the grounds that federal officials had failed to represent the tribe's interests. After lengthy negotiations, the existing Cheyenne contracts were nullified, new federal coal leases were signed, and the tribe received millions of dollars in compensation for lost revenue, legal costs, and environmental damage. Cheyenne leader Allen Rowland captured the mood of energy producing Indian tribes by saying, "We don't negotiate with the companies until they tear those leases up in front of us and burn them. And we can start over on our terms, not theirs." The Black Mesa and Northern Cheyenne problems inspired twenty-six tribes of the northern plains to form the Native American Natural

Resources Development Federation to establish fair prices and tribal controls "on their terms" and not those of the energy companies.

Because the Northern Cheyenne coal reserves have been estimated at between 20 and 50 billion tons, and because coal remains today a valuable source of energy in the United States, Northern Cheyenne tribal leaders continue to face pressure to adopt mining development from both big energy companies and Northern Cheyenne tribal members. For example, former councilman Danny Sioux promotes coal mining as "the only option we have" to deal with "tremendous social problems." Yet, a number of Cheyennes reject that idea. Lance Hughes tells of how his ancestors died defending their homeland. "Our reservation," he wrote, "thus represents the blood and tears of our grandparents, who willingly gave their lives so that we might live here." He argued that strip mining would devastate Northern Cheyenne lands. Cheyenne leaders are trying to find a middle ground between the positions of Sioux and Hughes. Eugene Little Coyote, current president of the Northern Cheyenne tribe, stated that, "The Tribe wants to ensure that its economic development is environmentally sound and culturally appropriate to preserve its beautiful homelands."

Whether or not the Northern Cheyennes open up their reservation to industrial development, they still have to defend their environment from encroachment from neighboring industrial projects. The reservation is surrounded by five huge strip mines, power plants, transmission lines, and several hundred methane wells, with up to sixteen thousand new methane wells under consideration by utilities and mining companies. Northern Cheyenne environmental campaigns include protecting the air that covers the reservations, which had become polluted by Montana's largest power plant, called Colstrip, and by the neighboring coal mines that fuel Colstrip. The tribe has established three mountaintop air-quality monitoring stations to ensure that these outside businesses don't violate the

Geri Small, who was the first woman to be elected president of the Northern Cheyenne tribe in 2000, currently serves as the cochairperson for the Northern Cheyenne Sand Creek Massacre Project Site, which hopes to raise awareness about one of the most tragic events in U.S. history. Small is shown here testifying to the Senate Affairs Committee about health-care conditions on Indian reservations shortly after she was elected.

Northern Cheyennes' strict air-quality standards, which are classified as Class I Airshed, the highest federal level that require the same standards as national parks.

Now the Northern Cheyennes are developing a tough water-quality program that will employ "standards equal to or better than the federal and state standards," according to tribal water-quality technician Joe Walksalong, Jr. Gail Small has fought to protect her people's land and water for years. Small has focused recently on preserving the quality of Northern Cheyenne water resources, noting that "Cheyenne live all along the [Tongue] river. They bathe in the river, a ceremonial [place] for healing." One of a number of Native American women involved in environmental protection movements,

Small serves as the director of a group called Native Action, which has campaigned against a new coal mining and gasification proposal. Gail's sister is Geri Small, the first woman to be elected president of the tribal council. Geri Small argued that even though this new proposal would make Cheyenne "millionaires," she would rather "keep our homeland, keep it intact."

Without extensive mining operations, the Cheyennes pursue other business opportunities. The Northern Cheyennes and the Southern Cheyennes derive their incomes from various businesses, such as ranching and farming, in addition to non-agricultural jobs in service and professional industries. In Montana, Cheyennes own construction, retail, and food service businesses. There are no manufacturing enterprises on the reservation, in part because of poor roads and facilities. The Northern Cheyennes have initiated a program at the college called the Tribal Business Information Center to help tribal members who are interested in starting their own businesses. Members of the Northern Cheyenne Chamber of Commerce serve as mentors by helping Cheyennes write business plans, conduct market research, and plan inventory control. Many of the businesses that have resulted have been small home-based companies that sell leather goods and beadwork, thus integrating Cheyenne culture with commerce.

Like many Native American communities, the Cheyennes offer some form of gambling to create revenue to fund social services, educational scholarships, and economic development. Since 1992, the Northern Cheyennes' Charging Horse Casino in Montana has offered a variety of games like keno, poker, and electronic bingo. Charging Horse is Montana's largest casino, offering 125 gaming devices, a 300-seat bingo hall, as well as a restaurant. In the 1990s, the Oklahoma Cheyenne and Arapaho tribe opened two casinos, which have provided roughly 300 new jobs and generated about $7 million per year, according to the 2002 Harvard Project on American Indian Economic

Development report. The Cheyennes and Arapahos have used their casino revenue to pay for a tribal police force, help tribal members pay burial costs, start a tobacco store and a bus system, and assist families in buying homes or deal with family emergencies. While some Cheyenne-Arapahos are ambivalent about gaming operations, others see it as a cornerstone of their sovereignty and as a source of income for other forms of economic development. For example, Southern Cheyenne elder Eugene Blackbear argued that "We need to get on our own feet. The casino is the only way today to make money."

Southern Cheyenne-Arapahos have been promoting a casino operation plan for Colorado called "The Cheyenne Arapaho Homecoming Project." Tribal leaders, who first have to get approval from Colorado state officials, hope that the casino can generate more than $100 million, which would help pay for health care, college tuition, and better schools, and provide nearly 1,500 new full-time jobs. The project, which includes a proposed "Colorado Plains Indian Cultural Center," is linked to Cheyenne and Arapaho land claims in Colorado that seek redress for land taken during the nineteenth century. While some Cheyennes see the approval of the casino project as a form of belated justice, others object. Steve Brady, president of the Northern Cheyenne Sand Creek Descendants, said "A casino operation and its proceeds is not any means of justice or reparations settlement."

Like many people in rural America, the Cheyennes contend with social problems and unemployment. The Cheyennes suffer from diabetes and infant mortality rates that are higher than the American population at large, as well as from a lower life-expectancy rate. The challenge to address these problems in addition to high unemployment is not easy. They will confront these challenges in a Cheyenne way. Northern Cheyenne educator Richard Littlebear notes that "indigenous people could avoid alcoholism, drugs, and abuse in all of its physical and violent forms, perhaps through our own Native healing practices."

In facing these challenges and thus preserving their identity in the twenty-first century, the Cheyennes in Montana, Oklahoma, and Colorado will draw upon the strength of their nineteenth-century ancestors who survived massacres and separations. As the great Northern Cheyenne tribal leader John Woodenlegs put it in 1960, the Cheyennes fight hard to preserve their reservation because their grandfathers died to do the same. Adopting various elements of American culture, current Cheyenne tribal leaders continue to fight to create a Cheyenne future for their children and grandchildren.

The Cheyennes at a Glance

Tribe Cheyenne

Culture Area Great Plains

Traditional Geography Northern Cheyenne: Wyoming and southern Montana;
Southern Cheyenne: eastern Colorado and Kansas

Linguistic Family Algonquian

Current Population (2000) Southern Cheyenne-Arapaho: more than 11,000; Northern Cheyenne: less than 4,500

First European Contact René-Robert Cavelier, Sieur de La Salle, French, 1680

Federal Status Recognized; Northern Cheyennes have a reservation in southeastern Montana

Late 1600s	Cheyennes settle in Red River area between Minnesota and North Dakota.
c. 1825	Cheyennes begin to split into two groups; Cheyennes sign treaty with U.S. government.
1828	Southern Cheyennes begin trading with Charles and William Bent.
c. 1830	By this time, Cheyennes are expert horsemen.
1830s	Southern Cheyennes feud with the Pawnees.
1851	Cheyennes help to negotiate with U.S. officials at pan-tribal gathering at Fort Laramie, Wyoming. The Treaty of Fort Laramie sets the territorial boundaries of Plains Indian tribes, including the Cheyenne.
1864	November 29: Colorado militia invade Cheyenne camp at Sand Creek in southeastern Colorado and massacre more than 150 Cheyennes and Arapahos.
1865	The Southern Cheyennes agree to cede most of Colorado Territory to the U.S. government.
1868	U.S. troops led by George Armstrong Custer massacre Southern Cheyennes at their camp on the Washita River, killing Peace Chief Black Kettle in the process.
1876	Cheyenne soldiers along with the Sioux defeat Custer's army at the Battle of Greasy Grass (Battle of the Little Bighorn).
1878	Dull Knife leads flight of Northern Cheyennes from Indian Territory.
1884	A federal government executive order creates the Northern Cheyenne Reservation in Montana.
1891	A Federal Act of March 3, 1891, divides Southern Cheyenne-Arapaho land into 160-acre parcels, and authorizes the sale of remaining land to white settlers.
1900	Another federal government executive order expands the boundaries of the Northern Cheyenne Reservation to 440,000 acres.

1926   Northern Cheyennes accept Allotment—one of the last tribes to do so.

1927   Southern Cheyennes perform the Massaum ceremony for the last time.

1935   Northern Cheyennes adopt a constitution and by-laws under the aegis of the Indian Reorganization Act.

1960   Northern Cheyenne tribal council president John Woodenlegs initiates his land-consolidation program.

1975   Cheyenne-Arapaho Nation adopts a constitution and by-laws to regulate tribal affairs.

1978   Chief Dull Knife College offers its first course on the Northern Cheyenne Reservation.

1990   Native American Graves Protection and Repatriation Act adopted by Congress, with the assistance of Cheyenne activists.

1992   The Cheyennes win the right to repatriate the remains of Cheyenne victims of the Sand Creek Massacre from the Smithsonian Institution; Northern Cheyenne Ben Nighthorse Campbell elected to the U.S. Senate—the first Native American in more than sixty years.

2004   National Museum of the American Indian opens in Washington, D.C.; W. Richard West, Jr., a Southern Cheyenne peace chief, serves as first museum director.

adobe—A building material of straw and earth dried in the sun.

agent or Indian agent—A person appointed by the Bureau of Indian Affairs to supervise U.S. government programs on a reservation and/or in a specific region; after 1908 the title "superintendent" replaced "agent."

Algonkian—The Indian peoples living in the northeastern United States and east-central Canada whose languages are related and who share numerous cultural characteristics.

Allotment—A U.S. policy applied nationwide through the General Allotment Act of 1887, intended to bring Indians into the mainstream by breaking up tribally owned reservations and tribal governments. Each tribal member was given, or allotted, a tract of land for farming.

Bowstring Society or Bowstring Soldiers—One of five Cheyenne warrior societies. The others were called Fox, Elk, Shield, and Dog. Each society had distinctive styles of dress, dance, and song, as well as particular rituals and rules of behavior.

Bureau of Indian Affairs (BIA)—A U.S. government agency established in 1824 and assigned to the Department of the Interior in 1849. Originally intended to manage trade and other relations with Indians and especially to supervise tribes on reservations, the BIA is now involved in programs that encourage Indians to manage their own affairs and improve their educational opportunities and general social and economic well-being.

calumet—A long pipe ornamented with feathers and scalp locks, used in Cheyenne ceremonies.

clan—A multigenerational group that has a common identity, organization, and property and that claims descent from a common ancestor. Because clan members consider themselves closely related, marriage within the clan is strictly prohibited.

counting coup—The act of touching an enemy with a crook-ended stick during battle, a sign of great prowess.

Dog Soldiers—The most powerful and feared of the five Cheyenne warrior societies.

Ghost Dance religion or Ghost or Spirit Dance—A religious movement that spread among Indians during the late 1880s centering on the belief that non-Indian newcomers would disappear and the Indians' traditional world would return if they enacted certain rituals, including dance movements performed for days at a time.

heum—A special seat reserved for the Sweet Medicine Chief inside the council tepee. It signified his position as representative of the earth-governing deity.

Indian Gaming Regulatory Act (IGRA)—Congress passed the IGRA in 1988 to provide the statutory basis for the administration of Indian gaming businesses. The IGRA created the National Indian Gaming Commission to oversee these businesses.

Indian Territory—An area in the south-central United States where the U.S. government wanted to resettle Indians from other regions, especially the eastern states. In 1907, the territory became the State of Oklahoma.

kinnikinnick—Tobacco, bark, dried leaves, herbs; and buffalo bone marrow blended together for smoking..

massa'ne—The comical antics of dancers dressed like animals in the Massaum Dance.

Native American Graves Protection and Repatriation Act (NAGPRA)—The legislation, passed in 1990, established new codes for protecting Native American gravesites and set guidelines for federal agencies and museums receiving federal funding to return sacred objects, ancestral remains, or cultural patrimony (defined as objects "having ongoing historical, traditional, or cultural importance, central to the Native American group or culture itself")

parfleche—A folded, rectangular container made of rawhide, used for storing dried foods, blankets, and clothing.

peyote—A cactus native to the southwestern United States and northern Mexico. The buttons of the cactus are sometimes eaten as part of Indian religious ceremonies.

Quakers—The familiar name for members of the Religious Society of Friends, a mystical and pacifist group founded in England by George Fox in the seventeenth century. Quakers were active in efforts to help Indians during the nineteenth century.

Quillers' Society—An exclusive women's group skilled in quill embroidery. The Quiller's Society supervised and instructed others in making quilled robes and observed certain rituals.

Renewal of the Medicine Arrows—An elaborate religious rite meant to renew the four Sacred Arrows and to unify the tribe.

Sun Dance—A religious rite highlighted by ceremonial dancing, it symbolized renewal of the world and often included self-torture.

tepee—A conical dwelling of the Plains tribes that consisted of a circular framework of poles joined at the top and covered with animal hides.

treaty—A contract negotiated between representatives of the United States and one or more Indian tribes. Treaties dealt with surrender of political independence, peaceful relations, land sales, boundaries, and related matters.

tribe—A type of society consisting of a community or group of communities that occupy a common territory and are related by bonds of kinship, language, and shared traditions.

Books

Afton, Jean, et al. *Cheyenne Dog Soldiers: A Ledgerbook History of Coups and Combat.* Niwot, Colo.: University Press of Colorado, 2000.

Ashabranner, Brent. *Morning Star, Black Sun.* New York: Dodd, Mead & Company, 1982.

Berthrong, Donald J. *The Cheyenne and Arapaho Ordeal.* Norman, Okla.: University of Oklahoma Press, 1976.

———. *The Southern Cheyennes.* Norman, Okla.: University of Oklahoma Press, 1963.

Bonner, T.D. *The Life and Adventures of James P. Beckwourth.* New York: Alfred A. Knopf, 1931.

Boye, Alan. *Holding Stone Hands: On the Trail of the Cheyenne Exodus.* Lincoln, Nebr.: University of Nebraska Press, 1999.

Fowler, Loretta. *Tribal Sovereignty and the Historical Imagination: Cheyenne-Arapaho Politics.* Lincoln, Nebr.: University of Nebraska Press, 2002.

Grinnell, George Bird. *The Fighting Cheyennes.* Norman, Okla.: University of Oklahoma Press, 1956.

Hatch, Thom. *Black Kettle: The Cheyenne Chief Who Sought Peace but Found War.* New York: Wiley, 2004.

Hoebel, E. Adamson. *The Cheyennes: Indians of the Great Plains.* New York: Holt, Rinehart and Winston, 1960.

Hoig, Stan. *The Battle of the Washita.* New York: Doubleday, 1976.

———. *The Peace Chiefs of the Cheyennes.* Norman, Okla.: University of Oklahoma Press, 1980.

———. *The Sand Creek Massacre.* Norman, Okla.: University of Oklahoma Press, 1961.

Hyde, George E., and Savoie Lottinville, eds. *Life of George Bent.* Norman, Okla.: University of Oklahoma Press, 1967.

Jablow, Joseph. *The Cheyenne in Plains Indian Trade Relations, 1795–1840.* Lincoln, Nebr.: University of Nebraska Press, 1994.

Little Coyote, Bertha, and Virginia Giglio. *Leaving Everything Behind: The Songs and Memories of a Cheyenne Woman.* Norman, Okla.: University of Oklahoma Press, 1997.

Llewellyn, Karl N., and E. Adamson Hoebel. *The Cheyenne Way*. Norman, Okla.: University of Oklahoma Press, 1941.

Mann, Henrietta. *Cheyenne-Arapaho Education 1871–1982*. Niwot, Colo.: University Press of Colorado, 1998.

Penoi, Charles. *No More Buffaloes*. Yukon, Okla.: Pueblo Publishing Press, 1981.

Powell, Peter J. *Sweet Medicine*. 2 vols. Norman, Okla.: University of Oklahoma Press, 1969.

Stands in Timber, John, and Margot Liberty. *Cheyenne Memories*, 2nd Edition. New Haven, Conn: Yale University Press, 1998.

Svingen, Orlan J. *The Northern Cheyenne Indian Reservation, 1877–1900*. Norman, Okla.: University of Oklahoma Press, 1993.

Websites

Bio of Former U.S. Senator Ben Nighthorse Campbell
http://bioguide.congress.gov/scripts/biodisplay.pl?index=C000077

Cheyenne-Arapaho Tribes of Oklahoma
http://www.cheyenneandarapaho.org/

Cheyenne Language Site
http://icemaid.virtualave.net/cheyenne2.html

Northern Cheyenne government
http://www.ncheyenne.net/tribalgovmt.htm

Sand Creek National Historic Site
http://www.nps.gov/sand/

Washita Battlefield National Historic Site
http://www.nps.gov/waba/

Northern Cheyenne Sand Creek Massacre Site Project
http://www.sandcreek.org/committee_who.htm

Abert, J.W., 36–38

agency life
attempts to return to home ranges, 82–84
BIA regulations and, 90–91
cattle raising and farming, 90
Dawes Act and, 87–88
economic progress and, 92–93
hardships after departure attempts, 84–86
life-improvement programs, 86–87
schooling and, 91–92
stripping of chiefs' power and, 89–90
white settlement of lands, 88–89

alcoholism, 30–35

Algonkian people, 8

Alights-on-the-Cloud (chief), 42, 43

American Religious Freedom Act (1978), 98

Amos Bad Heart Buffalo (artist), 80

Anthony, Scott J., 50

anti-Indian sentiment, 60

Arapaho-Cheyenne Reservation, 88–89

Assiniboines, 4, 9, 40

Atkinson, Henry (general), 24–25

Autry Museum of Western Heritage in Los Angeles, 98

Battle of Adobe Walls, 71

Battle of Little Bighorn (1876), 76–80

Battle of Wolf Creek, 27–28

Beckwourth, Jim, 30

Bell, J.R. (captain), 24

Bent, Charles, 22–23

Bent, Charlie, 53

Bent, George, 23, 52, 53, 70

Bent, William, 22–23, 45, 57

Benteen, Frederick (captain), 64, 77–79

Bent's Fort, 22–24, 27, 28, 31

Bent's New Fort, Treaty at (1860), 46

BIA (Bureau of Indian Affairs), 57, 75, 90–91, 92

Big Bellies (Gros Ventres), 1–6

Black Hawk (chief), 10

Black Hills (South Dakota), 76

Black Kettle (chief)
concessions by, 60
death of, 63–64
leadership of, 46, 53, 55, 62
speeches by, 49–50, 57–58

Bloodless Third, 50–51

Bob-tailed Horse (chief), 32, 34

"body snatching," 100

Bonner, T.D., 34–35

Bowstring Society, 11, 20, 25

Boys and Girls Club, 105

Bozeman Trail, 75

Brady, Steve, 112

Brave Wolf (chief), 79

Breakout Memorial Run, 101–102

Bridger, Jim, 40–41

Buell, George P. (colonel), 72

buffalo herds, 2–3, 7

buffalo-hide scraper, 15

Bull Bear (chief), 33, 49, 56, 70, 71

Bull Hump (chief), 26

Bureau of Indian Affairs (BIA), 57, 75, 90–91, 92

calumet, defined, 5–6

Campbell, Ben Nighthorse, 98–99

Camp Supply, 62, 64, 65, 70–71, 83

Camp Weld (Denver), 49

Carlisle Indian School (Pennsylvania), 91

Carr, E.A. (major), 65

Carson, Kit, 22–23, 27, 57

casinos, 111–112

Catlin, George (artist), 13, 25

celebrations. See powwows of twenty-first century

ceremonies. See rituals

Chaa tribe, 8

challenges of future, 112–113

Charging Horse Casino (Montana), 111

chastity of women, 16–17, 36

Cheyenne-Arapaho Business Committee, 96

Cheyenne-Arapaho cessation pact
(1891), 89, 96
"The Cheyenne Arapaho Homecoming
Project," 112
Cheyenne-Arapaho Reservation
(Oklahoma country), 88–89
Cheyenne-Arapaho separation initiatives, 96–97
*The Cheyenne Indians: Their History
and Way of Life* (Grinnell), 12
Cheyennes
background, 6–7
character of, 8–9, 24–25, 38–39
division of (Northern and
Southern), 22, 94–96
enemies of, 25–27
horses and, 9, 10, 90, 91
as hunters, 9, 10–11
language of, 102–103, 104
life of, 38–39
meeting with Gros Ventres and
Mandans, 1–6
migration of, 21–22
as warriors, 10–11
See also twenty-first century
Cheyennes
The Cheyenne Way (Llewellyn and
Hoebel), 12
Chief Dull Knife College, 102–105
chiefs, qualities of, 12–14
chiefs of the Cheyenne
Alights-on-the-Cloud, 42–43
Black Hawk, 10
Bob-tailed Horse, 32, 34
Brave Wolf, 79
Bull Bear, 33, 49, 56, 70, 71
Bull Hump, 26
Dull Knife, 74, 75, 80–81, 83–84
Gray Beard, 71, 73
High-backed Wolf, 12–13, 24, 25
Lame White Man, 79
the Lance, 20
Lean Bear, 46, 47–48, 49
Little Bear, 52
Little Chief, 43, 84–86, *85*

Little Moon, 24
Little Robe, 62, 65, 87
Little Wolf, 46, 74, 75, 82, 83
Medicine Arrows, 65, 70, 71
Minimic, 65
Old Bark, 32, 36, 37
Old Crow, 89, 90
Old Wolf, 34–35
One-Eye, 49, 53
Porcupine Bear, 34–35
Roman Nose, 42, 61
Slim Face, 33–35
Standing in the Water, 47
Stone Calf, 69, 70, 87
Tall Bear, 46
Tall Bull, 65–66
War Bonnet, 47
White Antelope, 42, 43, 46
White Horse, 65–66
Yellow Lodge, 33
Yellow Wolf, 22, 27, 36
See also Black Kettle; Left Hand
Chisholm, Jesse, 57
Chivington, John M. (colonel), 48,
50–54
Clark, William, 2, 20
Cleveland, Grover, 87
clothing, 16
coalfields, discovery of, 92, 108–110
colleges and universities, tribal,
102–105
Colley, Samuel G., 47
Colorado as homeland, 97
Colorado Gold Rush (1859), 42, 45
Colstrip, 109
Comanches, battle with, 27
Concho, Oklahoma, 96
Connor, P.E., 51
Consol (Consolidation Coal Company)
offer, rejection of, 108
council meetings, 14
councils, peace, 27, 37–38, 41, 43, 57
counting coup, 11
courtship procedure, 39
Crook, George (general), 76

Crossland, George, 92
Culbertson, Thaddeus A., 39
culture, attacks on preservation of, 89–91, 93
Custer, Boston, 77
Custer, George Armstrong (lieutenant colonel)
  in attack on Black Kettle (1864), 63–64
  Battle of Little Bighorn (1876) and, 7, 76–80
  leadership of, 58–59
  in rescue of white women (1869), 64–65
Custer, Tom, 77
Custer's last stand
  Custer's march, 76–78
  Darlington Agency site, 68–70
  destitution of tribe after, 80–81
  Fetterman Massacre, 75
  hostilities between Indians and U.S., 70–71
  Little Bighorn battle, 78–79
  Northern Cheyenne resistance, 73–75
  overtures by U.S., 75–76
  Sheridan's campaign, 71–73
  U.S. revenge for Little Bighorn, 79–80

Daily National Intelligencer, 25
dances, 106
  See also rituals
Darlington Agency, 56, 68–70, 81
Darlington, Brinton, 68–70
Dawes Act of 1887, 87–88
diseases brought by whites, 30, 70, 112
Dog Soldiers
  attacks on wagon trains by, 49
  characteristics of, 11–12
  disbanding of, 66–67
  Medicine Lodge Creek Treaty and, 60
  power of, 55
  warrior bands of, 58, 65, 87
domestic chores of women, 14–16

Dull Knife (chief), 74, 75, 80–81, 83–84
Dull Knife Community College, 102–105
dwellings. See tepees
Dyer, D.B., 87

Eayre, George S., 48–49
economic progress, 111
education, importance of, 91–92, 102–105
1825, Treaty of, 13, 24–25
Elk club, 11
Elliott, Joe (major), 64
English language, value of, 102
enrollment of reservations, 96, 192
Erect Horns, 18
Evans, John, 48–49, 50

farming as occupation, 90
Fetterman, W.J. (lieutenant), 75
Fetterman Massacre, 75
Fillmore, Millard, 43
Fitzpatrick, Thomas (agent), 40–41
food gathering, 14–15
Forsyth, George A. (colonel), 60–61
Fort Cobb, Oklahoma, Indian sanctuary, 62
Fort Crevecoeur, 8
Fort Laramie, Treaty of, 40–43, 44
Fort Sill Reservation, Oklahoma, 65, 71
Fort William. See Bent's Fort
Fox club, 11
Frémont, John Charles, 28–29
future challenges, 112–113

Gall (Sioux warrior), 79
gaming operations, 111–112
garments sewn by women, 16
Garrard, Lewis, 38–39
General Allotment Act. See Dawes Act of 1887
Ghost Dance religion, 88, 89
Gibbon, John (general), 76
gold prospectors, 45–46
Grant, Ulysses S., 67, 76

Gray Beard (chief), 71, 73
Greenwood, A.B., 46
Grierson, Benjamin, 65
Grinnell, G.B., 12
Gros Ventres (Big Bellies), 1–6, 40

Hamilton, Bill, 29
Hampton Institute (Virginia), 91
Hancock, Winfield Scott (major general), 58
Harjo, Susan, 98, 100
Hazen, William B. (general), 62
Hennessey, Patrick, 71
Henry, Alexander, 2, 6
heum, 14
He Who Walks with His Toes Turned Out (Wan-es-sah-ta), 42
Hidatsas, 1–2
High-backed Wolf (chief), 12–13, 24, 25
history, preservation of, 93, 101–102
Hoebel, E.A., 12
Hoffman, Archie, 97
homelands other than reservations, 97–98
Horse Creek, 40–41
horses, 9, 10, 90, 91
Hughes, Lance, 109

Indian Country Today (newspaper), 98
Indian Reorganization Act (1935), 96
industrial development controversy, 109
infant mortality, 112
initiatives for separation (Cheyenne-Arapaho), 96–97

Jacobs, Marcianna Little Man, 97

Kearny, Stephen Watts (colonel), 36
Keeper of the Arrows, 17–18, 26
Kellogg, W.K., Foundation, 103
Kidder, Lyman, 59
kinnikinnick, 39

Lame White Man (chief), 79
the Lance (chief), 20
land consolidation program, 96, 107
language, preservation of, 102–103, 104
Laramie, Wyoming, confrontation (1856), 44–45
La Salle, René-Robert Cavelier, Sieur de, 8
Lean Bear (chief), 46, 47–48, 49
Leavenworth, Jesse, 57, 59
Lee, Jesse M. (captain), 87
Left Hand (Arapaho chief), 46, 53
Lewis, Meriwether, 2, 20
The Life and Adventures of James P. Beckwourth (Bonner), 34–35
Lincoln, Abraham, 48, 49
Little Arkansas, Treaty of, 58
Little Bear (chief), 52
Littlebear, Richard, 102–103, 112
Little Bighorn, Battle of, 7, 76–79
Little Chief (chief), 43, 84–86, 85
Little Moon (chief), 24
Little Robe (chief), 62, 65, 87
Little Wolf (chief), 46, 74, 75, 82, 83
Llewellyn, K.N., 12
Lone Bear, Lee, 101–102
Lone Tepee rites, 18–19
Long, Stephen H., 24

Mackenzie, Charles, 2, 6
Mackenzie, Ranald S. (colonel), 72, 80
Mandans, 1–2, 40
Mann, Henrieta, 97–98
marriage ceremony, 17
massacre on Sand Creek. *See* Sand Creek Massacre
Medicine Arrows (chief), 65, 70, 71
Medicine Arrows ceremony, 18–19, 60, 89
Medicine Lodge Creek, Treaty of (1867), 59–60, 68
membership rolls (Red Cloud Agency), 75
Miles, John D., 71, 82, 86–87
Miles, Nelson A. (colonel), 72, 83, 87

military societies, 11–12, 55
Minimic (chief), 65
mining, strip, 92, 109
Missouri River Indian federation, 1
Mitchell, D.D., 42
modesty of women, 16–17, 36
Morgan, Anna, 65
Morning Star Institute, 98
"The Multiplier," 18

National Museum of the American
    Indian Act (1989), 98, 99
Native American Graves Protection
    and Repatriation Act (NAGPRA),
    98, 100–101
Native American Rights Fund, 97
natural resources, preservation of,
    106–109
New York Times, 64
North, Frank and Luther, 65
Northern Cheyenne Reservation
    (Montana), 94–96, 95
Northern Cheyennes
    attacks by, 73–75
    President Grant and, 75
    prosperity and, 92
    retaliation by U.S. on, 79–81
    split with Southern Cheyennes, 22,
        25, 39
    in twenty-first century, 94–96
    Twiss treaty of 1859 and, 46
Northern Cheyenne Sand Creek
    Descendants, 112
Northern Cheyenne Sand Creek
    Massacre Project Site, 110
Northern Cheyenne Tribal Council, 96
North Platte Agency treaty, 46
North West Trading Company, 2

Oklahoma Territory, 89
Old Bark (chief), 32, 36, 37
Old Crow (chief), 89, 90
Old Wolf (chief), 34–35
One-Eye (chief), 49, 53

Pawnee Killer (Lakota chief), 59
Pawnees, battles with, 26–27, 36
peace councils, 27, 37–38, 41, 43, 57
peyote, 89
Pine Ridge Agency, 80, 84
Platte Trail (Nebraska), 44
polygamy, 17, 89
population of reservations, 92, 96
Porcupine Bear (chief), 34–35
powwows of twenty-first century,
    105–106
preservation of past, 93, 101–102
"Pretty Encampment" (Cheyenne vil-
    lage), 38
proclamation by Governor Evans, 49
prospectors, gold, 45–46

Quakers, 67, 68–70, 71
Quillers' Society, 16

rattles, ceremonial, 5, 6
Redcherries, Carol, 98
Red Cloud Agency, 74, 75
Rendlebrock, Joseph (captain), 83
Renewal of the Medicine Arrows cere-
    mony, 18–19, 60, 89
Reno, Marcus (major), 77–79
repatriation movement, 100–101
"The Reproducer," 18
Republican River, 45, 48, 55
reservation life. See agency life
rituals
    Ghost Dance, 88, 89
    Medicine Arrows ceremony, 18–19,
        89
    powwows of today, 105–106
    Scalp Dance, 36
    Sun Dance ceremony, 17, 18–20, 89
Roman Nose (chief), 42, 61
Rowland, Allen, 108
Ruxton, George, 38–39

Sacred Mountain, 18
Sage, Rufus, 33
Sand Creek Massacre

Black Kettle's peace request, 49–50
Chivington's betrayal and, 50–54
delegation to Washington, D.C., 47–48
hostilities on Santa Fe Trail, 44–45
intrusion by gold prospectors, 45–46
Little Bear's account of, 52
repatriation of victims' remains, 100–101
Sumner's retaliation, 45
trauma after the, 97
treaty at Bent's New Fort (1860), 46
Santa Fe Trail, conflicts on, 44–45, 47
Scalp Dance, 36
schooling, 91–92, 102–105
scraper, buffalo-hide, 15
separation initiatives (Cheyenne-Arapaho), 96–97
Seventh Cavalry, Custer's, 76–79
Sheridan, Philip H. (general), 60, 61, 64, 71, 87
Sheridan's campaign, 71–73
She Who Bathes Her Knees, 25
Shield club, 11
Sioux, Danny, 109
Sioux nation, 8–9, 77
Slim Face (chief), 33–35
Small, Gail, 110–111
Small, Geri (president of Northern Cheyennes), 110–111
Smith, Jack, 53
Smith, John Simson, 38, 40–41, 50, 53, 57, 70
Smoky Hill meeting (1864), 49
Snake incident at Horse Creek, 41
Southern Cheyennes
    Chief Stone Calf and, 69, 70
    end of reign for, 73
    Pawnees and, 26–27
    poverty and prejudice suffered by, 92
    split with Northern Cheyennes, 22, 39
    treaty at Bent's New Fort and, 46–47
    in twenty-first century, 96–97

Southern Plains Indian chiefs' delegation, 47
Spotted Tail Agency, 75
Standing in the Water (chief), 47
Steele, James, 57
St. Louis, Slim Face and, 33–35
Stone Calf (chief), 69, 70, 87
Story of birds and beasts, 34–35
strip mining, 92, 109
Sully, Alfred (general), 61
Sumner, E.V. "Bull of the Woods," 45
Sun Dance ceremony, 17, 18–20, 89
surveyors, U.S. government, 70–71
Sweet Medicine Bundle, 14
Sweet Medicine Chief, 14

Tall Bear (chief), 46
Tall Bull (chief), 65–66
taxation, illegal, 89
tepees, 4, 7, 9, 38
Terry, Alfred H. (major general), 76–79
tools used by women, 15, 16
torture, ritual, 19
traders, unfair practices of, 31–33
traditions, preservation of, 93, 101–102
travois, defined, 4
Treaty at Bent's New Fort (1860), 46
treaty council (1867), 59–60
Treaty of 1825, 13, 24–25
Treaty of Fort Laramie, 40–43, 44
Treaty of Little Arkansas, 58
Treaty of Medicine Lodge Creek (1867), 59–60, 68
Tribal College Journal of American Indian Higher Education, 102
tribal colleges, 102–105
the Tsetschestahase in the twenty-first century. *See* twenty-first century Cheyennes
Tsis-tsis'-tas (the people), 8
twenty-first century Cheyennes
    casinos and, 111–112
    challenges of future, 112–113
    economic progress and, 111
    environmental concerns of, 108–111

homelands of, 97–98
language of, 102–103, 104
leadership of, 98–100, 99
natural resources and, 106–109
overview, 94–96, 95
powwows of the, 105–106
preservation of past and, 101–102
repatriation demands of, 100–101
tribal colleges and, 102–105
women of the, 98
Twiss, Thomas S., 46
Two Bulls, Lynette, 102

unemployment, rates of, 112
U.S. Army-Cheyenne confrontation, 44

Wah-to-yah and the Taos Trail
 (Garrard), 38–39
Walksalong, Joe, Jr., 110
Wan-es-sah-ta (He Who Walks with
 His Toes Turned Out), 42
War Bonnet (chief), 47
water quality programs, 110–111
West, W. Richard, 99–100, 106
White, Sarah, 65
White Antelope (chief), 42, 43, 46

White Horse (chief), 65–66
Whiteman, Montoya, 97–98
Whiteman, Philip, Jr., 101
whites
 as bad omens, 20
 blessings brought by, 30
 broken agreements of, 42, 48
 diseases brought by, 30–31
 unfair trading practices of, 31–33
 See also entries beginning with Battle;
  entries beginning with Treaty
Wind River Reservation (Northern
 Arapahos), 96
W.K. Kellogg Foundation, 103
women, 14–17, 36, 70, 98
Woodenlegs, John, 96, 107, 113
Woodson, A.E., 89
Wovoka (medicine man), 88
Wynkoop, Edward W., 49, 50, 58

Xammaa-vo'estaneo'o (Cheyenne
 word), 106

Yellow Lodge (chief), 33
Yellow Wolf (chief), 22, 27, 36
youth powpow, 105

PICTURE CREDITS

page:

3: Western History Collections, The University of Oklahoma Library

5: © Werner Forman/Art Resource, NY

13: Photo Courtesy of National Museum of American Art, Smithsonian Institution

15: Denver Art Museum

17: Photograph Courtesy of Smithsonian Institution, National Museum of the American Indian

23: Colorado Historical Society

28: © George H.H. Huey/CORBIS

31: Denver Art Museum

37: Western History Collections, The University of Oklahoma

42: Photo Courtesy of Smithsonian Institution

47: Library of Congress, LC-USZ62-11880

51: Colorado Historical Society

56: Photo Courtesy of Smithsonian Institution

63: © Danny Lehman/CORBIS

66: Library of Congress, LC-DIG-cwpbh-03110

69: Western History Collections, University of Oklahoma Libraries

74: Photo Courtesy of Smithsonian Institution

80: Newberry Library, Chicago

85: Photo Courtesy of Smithsonian Institution

88: Western History Collections, University of Oklahoma Libraries

95: © Peter Lamb

99: © MARIO TAMA/AFP/Getty Images

106: Rob Stapleton/Dembinsky Photo Associates

110: Associated Press, *Billings Gazette*

A: Department of Material Culture, Colorado Historical Society, #CHS-X20039

B: Department of Material Culture, Colorado Historical Society, #CHS-X3298

C: Department of Material Culture, Colorado Historical Society, #CHS-X20022

D: Department of Material Culture, Colorado Historical Society, #CHS-X2831

E: © Werner Forman/CORBIS

F: © Werner Forman/CORBIS

G: © Werner Forman/Art Resource, NY

H: © Aldo Tutino/Art Resource, NY

Cover: © Christie's Images/CORBIS

Stan Hoig is Emeritus Professor of Journalism at Central State University in Edmond, Oklahoma, and has written extensively on the Cheyennes. His books include: *The Battle of the Washita, The Peace Chiefs of the Cheyenne,* and *The Sand Creek Massacre.*

Paul C. Rosier received his Ph.D. in American History from the University of Rochester, with a specialty in Native American History. His first book, *Rebirth of the Blackfeet Nation, 1912–1954,* was published by the University of Nebraska Press in 2001. In November 2003, Greenwood Press published *Native American Issues* as part of its Contemporary American Ethnic Issues series. Dr. Rosier has also published articles on Native American topics in the *American Indian Culture and Research Journal,* and the *Journal of American Ethnic History.* In addition, he was coeditor of *The American Years: A Chronology of United States History.* He is Assistant Professor of History at Villanova University, where he also serves as a faculty advisor to the Villanova Native American Student Association.

Ada E. Deer is the director of the American Indian Studies program at the University of Wisconsin–Madison. She was the first woman to serve as chair of her tribe, the Menominee Nation, the first woman to head the Bureau of Indian Affairs in the U.S. Department of the Interior, and the first American Indian woman to run for Congress and secretary of state of Wisconsin. Deer has also chaired the Native American Rights Fund, coordinated workshops to train American Indian women as leaders, and championed Indian participation in the Peace Corps. She holds degrees in social work from Wisconsin and Columbia.